We Are Invincibles

The Incredible Story of Bradman's 1948 Team

Anindya Dutta

Special Feature:

'My Encounters with the Invincibles'

Kersi Meher-Homji

This book is dedicated to the two Invincible spirits in my life who inspire me every moment of every day with their love, patience and immense faith in me as a human being.

To my wife Anisha

And

My canine daughter Olu

Contents

1. Introduction — 7
2. The Battle for Nottingham — 13
3. Lording it over England — 33
4. Bradman's 50th Test — 51
5. The Greatest Test Match — 67
6. Forever Invincibles — 87
7. My Encounters with the Invincibles — 105
8. Appendix – The 1948 Ashes Series — 115

Introduction

I fell in love with cricket and its history at an early age, watching India come back from a 0-2 deficit to beat the mighty West Indies at the Eden Gardens in Calcutta, sitting alongside my father and listening to the exploits of great Indian players at the lunch and tea breaks. Between the Indian names that I heard for the first time over those five days of fascinating cricket, was a very non-Indian one, mentioned every time a beautiful shot was played – Don Bradman. The name stuck in my impressionable young mind.

As the years went by, the stories of India's twin triumphs of 1971 over the West Indies and England were a source of intense fascination. In 1983 when Kapil Dev took that incredible catch in the outfield to dismiss Vivian Richards at Lord's and then held aloft the Prudential World Cup, for me and millions of my generation across India, the place that cricket occupied in our hearts and minds expanded exponentially.

As Indian cricket grew in confidence and stature, my own cricketing horizons widened to include shores far away where the battle for cricket supremacy had been waging between Australia and England for almost 150-years. The exploits of Fred 'The Demon Bowler' Spofforth and the battles with the mountainous personality of Dr. WG Grace became a source of intense fascination.

More than a hundred years before limited overs cricket made the slower ball fashionable, Fred Spofforth was perfecting it. The Guardian would write: "Spofforth varies his pace in the most remarkable way, at one time sending down a tremendously fast ball and at another almost a slow one." In his own writing, Spofforth would say: "Variation is only any use if you learn to hide it. The sole object in variation is to make the batsman think the ball is faster or slower than it really is."

As importantly, Spofforth's role in how this contest between Australia and England came to be called the Ashes was a source of endless fascination for me.

At the Oval in 1882, WG Grace earned the ire of Spofforth by slyly running an Australian batsman Sammy Jones out when the batsman had deemed the ball 'dead'. At the break, there was an exchange between Spofforth and Grace which ended acrimoniously, notwithstanding the high esteem in which the two held each other. Spofforth stormed out of the English changing room telling Grace: "This will cost you the match." Then back in his own dressing room, with England needing 85 runs to win the match in the last innings, the story goes that Spofforth roared to his teammates, "I swear to you, England will not win this…..this thing can be done."

He took the first two wickets off successive balls to leave England reeling at 15 for 2. Then, with England at 66 for 5, Spofforth was brought back into the attack. He ran through the side in a remarkable spell of fast bowling, with his last 11 overs fetching 4 wickets for 2 runs, including 3 wickets in 4 balls.

This then was the truly magnificent spell of bowling that launched *The Ashes* contest between Australia and England. It was after this defeat that the *Sporting Times* carried a mock obituary mourning the death of English cricket, promising that "the body will be cremated and the ashes taken to Australia.", ensuring that Fred Spofforth's name would be remembered alongside WG Grace's more than a century later as the men who laid the memorable foundations of the *Gentleman's Game*.

The Bodyline series of 1933 was the stuff movies are made of. An English captain - Douglas Jardine, determined to neutralise the impact of Donald Bradman; Harold Larwood – one of the greatest fast bowlers the world has known, employed as the tool to achieve this; Bodyline – the most controversial strategy ever implemented on a cricket field. It would bring into question whether cricket was truly (or had ever been or would again be) the Gentleman's Game.

But nothing fascinated me more than the journey to Invincibility of Don Bradman's 1948 Australian team to England. The more I read about it, the more I wanted to know. At one point it became an obsession. And then I passed the point of no return when I acquired a pristine copy of the 1948 Australian side's 'Team Sheet', signed be every single member of the *Invincibles*. As I passed my hands over the signatures of Bradman and his boys, analysed the bold strokes, the scrawled names, the lazy but ingenious rubber stamping of his signature by Sidney Barnes, the characters jumped out at me through the long dried ink on that page. I had to tell the story.

Every character on that tour was special in his own way. Don Bradman – in his last series as player and captain of Australia, obsessed with coming back undefeated, something no Australian captain had ever achieved. Keith Miller – war pilot, flamboyant personality, ladies' man, fearsome fast bowler and a powerful batsman. Neil Harvey – youngest member of the squad, fated to be the successor of the Don. Len Hutton – one of the greatest batsmen of all time, dropped inexplicably for a Test from an English side weakened by the effects of a long war. And of course the story of how Bradman's average remained at 99.94, the most famous number in the history of cricket.

This book is my tribute to Bradman's Invincibles. It is a story that has been told before, but what I have tried to do here is weave the story around the tour of the characters who played such an important part, the post-war England that hosted the tour not long after the most devastating conflict in the history of mankind had ended, and tell the fascinating story of how through it all the single thread that kept it all together was one man's determination to make history in a manner that would never again be possible.

Enjoy the story!

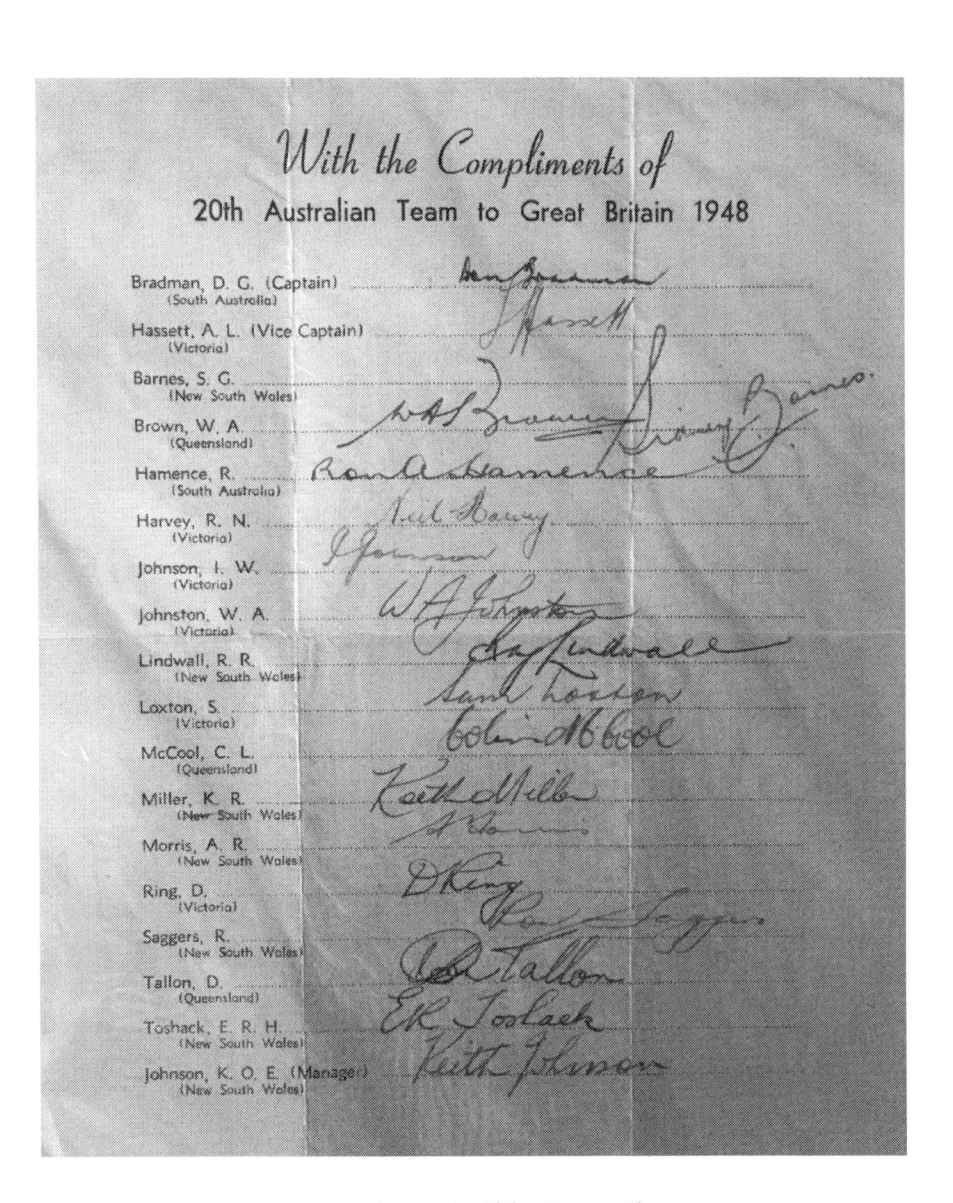

With the Compliments of
20th Australian Team to Great Britain 1948

Bradman, D. G. (Captain) (South Australia)	*[signature]*
Hassett, A. L. (Vice Captain) (Victoria)	*[signature]*
Barnes, S. G. (New South Wales)	*[signature]*
Brown, W. A. (Queensland)	*[signature]*
Hamence, R. (South Australia)	*[signature]*
Harvey, R. N. (Victoria)	*[signature]*
Johnson, I. W. (Victoria)	*[signature]*
Johnston, W. A. (Victoria)	*[signature]*
Lindwall, R. R. (New South Wales)	*[signature]*
Loxton, S. (Victoria)	*[signature]*
McCool, C. L. (Queensland)	*[signature]*
Miller, K. R. (New South Wales)	*[signature]*
Morris, A. R. (New South Wales)	*[signature]*
Ring, D. (Victoria)	*[signature]*
Saggers, R. (New South Wales)	*[signature]*
Tallon, D. (Queensland)	*[signature]*
Toshack, E. R. H. (New South Wales)	*[signature]*
Johnson, K. O. E. (Manager) (New South Wales)	*[signature]*

The *Invincibles* Team Sheet

The Battle for Nottingham

Isn't that Don Bradman over there? I would like to be introduced.

-- Winston Churchill, at a public gathering in 1948

In the summer of '48, Don Bradman led a formidable Australian team across the oceans with intent, with resolve, with enormous talent in their ranks, and with the dogged will to win all that they could. The stories around those 56 days on the voyage and the 112 days of brilliant cricket (of the 144 days spent on tour in Great Britain), have become the stuff of lore, taking on a life of their own in the telling and re-telling over the past 70-years.

After years of destruction and loss of human life in a Britain where the populace continued to face rationing, this Australian team brought back the joy of cricket at its very best. Bradman had announced before the tour that it was going to be his last and, combined with the Australians' swashbuckling style on the field and the swagger on and off it, this was a breath of fresh air to the thousands clamouring to get into the grounds to witness history being made. Attendance records would be broken that stand uncontested seven decades later.

While the result of the tour would not be uniformly pleasing to the peoples of the two nations, there is no doubt that the quality of the cricket was of the highest order.

The 1948 Australian Team to England

The Australian Team

The 1948 Australian team, besides Bradman, comprised Lindsay Hassett (vice-captain), Arthur Morris (co-opted selector), Sid Barnes, Bill Brown, Ron Hamence, Neil Harvey, Ian Johnson, Bill Johnston, Ray Lindwall, Sam Loxton, Colin

McCool, Keith Miller, Doug Ring, Ron Saggers, Don Tallon, and Ernie Toshack.

Since the resumption of cricket following World War II, Australia had played 11 Tests and had been unbeaten. In 1946–47, they won the five-Test series against England 3–0, and followed this with a 4–0 series win over India in the following season. All the Tests had been played at home, but the core of the team that sailed to England comprised of players who had been a part of this string of victories.

The agreed playing conditions were a big factor in team selection. England had agreed to make a new ball available after 55 six-ball overs in the Tests; a new ball was generally taken after every 200 runs, which usually took more than 55 overs to accumulate as per the strike rates of the time, so the rule change meant that a new ball was more frequently available. Unsurprisingly, the Australians chose a strong pace attack to form the core of the bowling.

The selection was however not easy. Chronic knee injuries had begun to hamper medium-pacer Ernie Toshack, and he only made the trip after a 3–2 vote by a medical panel. Leading paceman Ray Lindwall had been playing with an injured leg tendon. In addition, his foot drag during the delivery stride led to speculation about the legality of his bowling action. While the injury was tackled before the tour, Bradman, with his immense experience, advised his bowler to ensure that his foot was further behind the line than usual to avoid being no-balled, and to operate below full speed until the umpires were satisfied. It is a testimony to the efficacy of this advice that Lindwall was not hampered by a no-balling issue on the tour. Keith Miller had drawn Bradman's attention while playing the Victory Tests in 1945 for the Australian Services Team against England immediately after the war, and while Miller considered himself primarily a batsman, the captain saw enormous potential in his pace and movement. In the 1946-47 series at home, Miller had surprised himself with his penetration partnering Lindwall.

Lindwall and Miller were fearsome fast bowlers, with high pace and the ability to deliver menacing short-pitched bowling at the upper body of the batsmen. England had no pacemen to counter with the same tactics, Alec Bedser being the sole workhorse. At one stage during the tour, the short-pitched bowling of the Australians prompted England to drop Len Hutton from the team which further weakened the batting.

The batting line up was an embarrassment of riches with the likes of Hassett, Morris, Barnes, Hamence and future superstar teenaged Neil Harvey.

Hassett was already popular with the British public as much for his batting as for the stories from his time with the Allied Forces. There was the story of an 'irritating young subaltern' who, unimpressed with Hassett's cavalier attitude towards military discipline told him: "If you took the trouble to clean your rifle you might just manage to become a good soldier." Pat came Hassett's reply to the less than capable cricketer: "If you cleaned and oiled your cricket bat for twenty years, sir, you'd never score a run."

Lindsay Hassett

Then there was the favourite tale doing the rounds of a Hassett quip when he saw a Middle Eastern sheikh with his 199 wives: "One more and he's entitled to a new ball."

But rising above everyone in the team was the towering personality and stature of little Don Bradman.

The Australian journalist Andy Flanagan wrote about the anticipation of Bradman's arrival in England: "…cities, towns and hotels are beflagged, carpets set down, and dignitaries wait to extend an official welcome. He is the Prince of Cricketers." Bradman received hundreds of personal letters every day, and one of his dinner speeches was broadcast live, causing the BBC to take the unprecedented step of postponing the news bulletin. Following Bradman through the tour was the buzz about his clearly stated intention to become the first team to go back undefeated from the British Isles.

Bradman's words sum up how he felt about his 1948 team: "Knowing the personnel, I was confident that here, at last, was the great opportunity which I had longed for. A team of cricketers whose respect and loyalty were unquestioned, who would regard me in a fatherly sense and listen to my advice, follow my guidance and not question my handling of affairs … there are no longer any fears that they will query the wisdom of what you do. The result is a sense of freedom to

Bradman being given a poppy by a young lady

give full reign to your own creative ability and personal judgment."

The Battle for Nottingham

In the days of long travel across the seas followed by longer tours that lasted a few months, it was customary to play a number of first-class fixtures before the real battle started on the Test arena. In fact, the amount of cricket that teams had to play far exceeded the workload of modern players notwithstanding the many formats that exist today. On a typical tour of England, there was cricket played 6 days a week over a 5-month tour. Then there was the travel to and from matches on match days by train and bus.

So when the teams came to Robin Hood's Nottingham for the first Test, the Australians had already played 12 first-class matches, winning ten and drawing two. Eight of these victories had been by an innings and another by eight wickets. The intent was now clear by deed as it was by word.

With rain forecast, Bradman picked Ian Johnson the off spinner to exploit a wet wicket. The rest of the bowling line up was filled with his pacemen. Norman Yardley won the toss and elected to bat first to avoid having to deal with a deteriorating pitch in the fourth innings. If Bradman had won the toss he would have done the same. He would candidly admit later: "I am certain we won the 1948 Nottingham Test because I lost the toss."

Walking out to bat were Hutton and Washbrook, a pair that had put together three century partnerships against

Lindwall and Miller in 1946-47. Lindwall was cautious, conscious of his foot and cutting back on his pace by a quarter while Miller bowled at full tilt with no warm up. Facing up to Miller's second over, Hutton was slow to step forward and the ball took the edge. Australia had the first breakthrough as a pre-lunch downpour sent the players back to the pavilion.

When the players come back Edrich was dropped but Lindwall got Washbrook to hook one to Brown at the boundary. Before long, England was 46 for 4 and when Dennis Compton was bowled by Miller, half the English side had been dismissed for 48. This soon became 74 for 8 before Jim Laker and Alec Bedser came together with swinging bats and put on 89 to take England to a semi-respectable 165 all out.

Malcolm Knox in his book *Bradman's War* would quip: "England's 165 was worse than it should have been but better than it might have been." Laker was the highest scorer with 63. Bill Johnston ended with 5 for 36, the result of his accurate bowling using pace and swing in equal measure. At one stage his first two wickets in Test cricket had come without expensing a single run. Miller had 3 for 38.

The British press harboured no illusions about England's bowling strength. This was evident in the sweepstakes run in the press box which put Australia's likely score anywhere between 302 and 904.

Australian openers Morris and Barnes took the score to 73 before Laker removed Morris. Bradman came in and the score moved to 121 before Barnes at his score of 62 was caught by wicket-keeper Godfrey Evans with a one-handed diving effort. Bradman would say about the catch: "Evans' catching of Barnes was one of the most miraculous feats of recovery as well as acrobatics one would see in a long time." Miller was then dismissed for a duck by Laker. Brown didn't last long and then Lindsay Hassett joined Bradman at the crease.

Bradman had thus far not been entirely at ease. Alec Bedser employed a leg side field and kept attacking his pads. The Edrich replaced Laker and proceeded to bounce Bradman who got the first taste of what it might have been like for the English batsmen to face Lindwall and Miller without sightscreens, for none had been made available for the Test.

Bradman would later write: "English authorities are very casual about such details. They don't always appear to regard the player's requirements as Priority No. 1...it may enable a few more spectators to see the game – in other words it may add a few pounds to the gate money – but that won't compensate for somebody getting cracked on the head one day."

Edrich's bouncers were replaced by 17 overs of Barnett with every single ball pitching outside the leg stump with six fielders on the leg. Bradman watched Hassett deal with this negative bowling with hand on his hip and ankles crossed at the non-striker's end.

Barnes sitting in the pavilion wrote: "This is not bowling; it is not cricket at all. Just a waste of time." Hassett made no attempt to force the pace and Tiger O'Reilly, now a journalist rather unfairly wrote about his batting: "the most outstanding feature of the batting was the unlimited capacity as a crowd-boring agency." John Arlott was kinder: "Hassett made his runs so slowly that only his grace and concealed humour made his innings tolerable." For all the criticism, Hassett's final contribution was a valuable 137.

When Bradman finally raised his bat after 221 minutes at the crease, it was the slowest of the 29 centuries he would score in his career. That night, Tiger O'Reilly went to the Black Boy Hotel for a drink with Alec Bedser. Always generous with his advice, O'Reilly advised Bedser to move Hutton from leg slip to fine-leg, twelve yards from the bat, add a mid-on and a short leg, then bowl a faster ball into Bradman's left hip and rib cage.

In Bedser's second over of the morning, Bradman was gone for 138, glancing a ball between his left hip and rib cage to Hutton at short fine leg. Bedser waved to O'Reilly in the press box and the Australians went ballistic with accusations of betraying Bradman. It was all, however, a bit late. When the Australians were finally dismissed, they had amassed 509.

Hutton and Washbrook walked out needing to bat two days to save the Test. Washbrook was caught behind attempting a hook to a Miller bouncer on the leg side, and Edrich failed to read an Ian Johnson arm ball. John Arlott remarked: "The price of reserved tickets for the fifth day's play at once dropped several more points."

But without an injured Lindwall to pin him down, Len Hutton went on the offensive. Compton soon joined the party and they were scoring at more than a run a minute. To quote Arlott, "With the game apparently within their grasp, Australia were threatened by two great batsmen batting at their greatest." Keith Miller decided to try off-spin and was promptly hit for a flurry of fours by Hutton. Miller went back to his long run, fuming and muttering under his breath. Hutton had unwittingly unleashed the devil, as he would soon realise.

Miller didn't care that this was Nottingham, the home of Harold Larwood. The colliers of Nottingham had not forgiven Bradman and his men for what had happened to fellow collier Larwood, made the fall guy for Douglas Jardine's *Bodyline*. For the last thirty-five minutes of play that day he sent down an average of four bouncers an over at Hutton and Compton. This was Miller's version of Bodyline, in fading light, without sightscreens. Hutton would confess after retirement: "I did not fear being hit, but Miller was the exception. I never felt physically safe against him." Miller was booed, barracked, and physically threatened.

The next day Miller dismissed Hutton with an off-cutter then got Compton hit wicket while hooking, but by then he had scored 184 and England was 405 for 7. Eventually, England was all out for 441 leaving Australia to score 98 to win. With rain coming down heavily all over Nottingham but seemingly miraculously sparing the ground, and Bradman out for a duck in an exact repeat of the dismissal from the first innings, an unbeaten 64 from Sidney Barnes ensured an eight-wicket victory for the visitors.

But a match as dramatic as this could hardly end on such a sedate note. As Barnes hit Young for a four with Australia's score at 93 and sprinted into the pavilion picking up a stump on the way as a souvenir, he looked back to see all the English players and his partner waiting in their places. One of the players in the dressing room advised him to go back as Australia still needed a run. It was Hassett who would finally hit that winning run. A fuming Barnes was denied a stump as the English players made sure they picked up all six on their way to the pavilion.

Australia had a 1-0 lead and Bradman's lads had taken the first step on what would be a long journey to the Invincibles sobriquet that they would eventually earn.

Dennis Compton

Scorecard - 1st Test

England v Australia

Australia in British Isles 1948 (1st Test)

Venue	Trent Bridge, Nottingham on 10th, 11th, 12th, 14th, 15th June 1948 (5-day match)
Balls per over	6
Toss	England won the toss and decided to bat
Result	Australia won by 8 wickets
Umpires	F Chester, E Cooke
Close of play day 1	Australia (1) 17/0 (Barnes 6*, Morris 10*; 4 overs)
Close of play day 2	Australia (1) 293/4 (Bradman 130*, Hassett 41*; 134 overs)
Close of play day 3	England (2) 121/2 (Hutton 63*, Compton 36*; 51 overs)
Close of play day 4	England (2) 345/6 (Compton 154*, Evans 10*)

England first innings		Runs	Balls	Mins	4s	6s
L Hutton	b Miller	3	8	12	-	-
C Washbrook	c Brown b Lindwall	6	41	41	-	-
WJ Edrich	b Johnston	18	69	74	1	-
DCS Compton	b Miller	19	59	60	2	-

25

J Hardstaff	c Miller b Johnston	0	2	2	-	-
CJ Barnett	b Johnston	8	32	16	1	-
*NWD Yardley	lbw b Toshack	3	46	26	-	-
+TG Evans	c Morris b Johnston	12	24	18	2	-
JC Laker	c Tallon b Miller	63	97	101	6	-
AV Bedser	c Brown b Johnston	22	86	89	2	-
JA Young	not out	1	10	8	-	-
Extras	(5 b, 5 lb)					10
Total	(all out, 79 overs)					165

Fall of wickets:

1-9 (Hutton, 3.1 ov), 2-15 (Washbrook, 12.2 ov), 3-46 (Edrich, 27.3 ov), 4-46 (Hardstaff, 27.5 ov), 5-48 (Compton, 30.6 ov), 6-60 (Barnett, 39.3 ov), 7-74 (Evans, 45.6 ov), 8-74 (Yardley, 46.5 ov), 9-163 (Bedser, 75.5 ov), 10-165 (Laker, 79 ov)

Australia bowling	Overs	Mdns	Runs	Wkts	Wides	No-Balls
Lindwall	13	5	30	1	-	-
Miller	19	8	38	3	-	-
Johnston	25	11	36	5	-	-
Toshack	14	8	28	1	-	-
Johnson	5	1	19	0	-	-
Morris	3	1	4	0	-	-

Australia first innings		Runs	Balls	Mins	4s	6s
SG Barnes	c Evans b Laker	62	160	153	6	-
AR Morris	b Laker	31	90	121	3	-
*DG Bradman	c Hutton b Bedser	138	323	290	10	-
KR Miller	c Edrich b Laker	0	9	6	-	-
WA Brown	lbw b Yardley	17	62	58	1	-
AL Hassett	b Bedser	137	383	354	20	1
IWG Johnson	b Laker	21	51	38	3	-
+D Tallon	c and b Young	10	43	39	1	-
RR Lindwall	c Evans b Yardley	42	116	121	7	-
WA Johnston	not out	17	23	27	2	-
ERH Toshack	lbw b Bedser	19	39	18	3	-
Extras	(9 b, 4 lb, 1 nb, 1 w)					15
Total	(all out, 216.2 overs)					509

Fall of wickets:

1-73 (Morris, 31.5 ov), 2-121 (Barnes, 53.2 ov), 3-121 (Miller, 55.5 ov), 4-185 (Brown, 75.4 ov), 5-305 (Bradman, 136.3 ov), 6-338 (Johnson, 149.4 ov), 7-365 (Tallon, 166.1 ov), 8-472 (Hassett, 204.6 ov), 9-476 (Lindwall, 207.2 ov), 10-509 (Toshack, 216.2 ov)

England bowling	Overs	Mdns	Runs	Wkts	Wides		No-Balls
Edrich	18	1	72	0	1	-	
Bedser	44.2	12	113	3	-		1
Barnett	17	5	36	0	-	-	
Young	60	28	79	1	-	-	
Laker	55	14	138	4	-	-	
Compton	5	0	24	0	-	-	
Yardley	17	6	32	2	-	-	

England second innings		Runs	Balls	Mins	4s	6s
L Hutton	b Miller	74	181	168	11	-
C Washbrook	c Tallon b Miller	1	12	10	-	-
WJ Edrich	c Tallon b Johnson	13	64	43	2	-
DCS Compton	hit wkt b Miller	184	478	413	19	-
J Hardstaff	c Hassett b Toshack	43	127	101	6	-
CJ Barnett	c Miller b Johnston	6	28	33	-	-
*NWD Yardley	c and b Johnston	22	70	66	4	-
+TG Evans	c Tallon b Johnston	50	110	124	8	-
JC Laker	b Miller	4	11	16	-	-

AV Bedser	not out	3	18	20	-	-
JA Young	b Johnston	9	11	8	2	-
Extras	(12 b, 17 lb, 3 nb)					32
Total	(all out, 183 overs)					441

Fall of wickets:

1-5 (Washbrook, 2.6 ov), 2-39 (Edrich, 20.6 ov), 3-150 (Hutton, 66.2 ov), 4-243 (Hardstaff, 104.2 ov), 5-264 (Barnett, 115.4 ov), 6-321 (Yardley, 140.3 ov), 7-405 (Compton, 173.4 ov), 8-413 (Laker, 177.3 ov), 9-423 (Evans, 180.1 ov), 10-441 (Young, 183 ov)

Australia bowling	Overs	Mdns	Runs	Wkts	Wides	No-Balls
Miller	44	10	125	4	-	-
Johnston	59	12	147	4	-	-
Toshack	33	14	60	1	-	3
Barnes	5	2	11	0	-	-
Johnson	42	15	66	1	-	-

Australia second innings		Runs	Balls	Mins	4s	6s
SG Barnes	not out	64	101	87	11	-
AR Morris	b Bedser	9	32	32	1	-
*DG Bradman	c Hutton b Bedser	0	10	12	-	-

AL Hassett	not out	21	32	39	2 -
KR Miller	did not bat				
WA Brown	did not bat				
IWG Johnson	did not bat				
+D Tallon	did not bat				
RR Lindwall	did not bat				
WA Johnston	did not bat				
ERH Toshack	did not bat				
Extras	(2 lb, 1 nb, 1 w)				4
Total	(2 wickets, 28.3 overs)				98

Fall of wickets:

1-38 (Morris, 10.6 ov), 2-48 (Bradman)

England bowling	Overs	Mdns	Runs	Wkts	Wides		No-Balls
Bedser	14.3	4	46	2	-		1
Edrich	4	0	20	0	1	-	
Young	10	3	28	0	-	-	

--> Day 1 Lunch: England (1) 13/1 (Washbrook 6*, Edrich 3*; 5 overs)
--> Day 1 Tea: England (1) 75/8 (Laker 1*, Bedser 0*; 48 overs)
--> Day 2 Lunch: Australia (1) 104/1 (Barnes 51*, Bradman 19*; 46 overs)
--> Day 2 Tea: Australia (1) 215/4 (Bradman 78*, Hassett 15*; 94 overs)
--> Day 3 Lunch: Australia (1) 385/7 (Hassett 84*, Lindwall 9*; 177 overs)
--> Day 3 Tea: Australia (1) 509 all out
--> Day 4 Lunch: England (2) 191/3 (Compton 63*, Hardstaff 31*; 78 overs)
--> Day 4 Tea: England (2) 248/4 (Compton 97*, Barnett 0*; 107 overs)
--> Day 5 Lunch: England (2) 411/7 (Evans 41*, Laker 2*; 177 overs)
--> J Hardstaff made his last appearance in Test matches
--> CJ Barnett made his last appearance in Test matches
--> JC Laker (1) 50 in 78 balls, 63 minutes with 4 fours
--> JC Laker (1) passed his previous highest score of 55 in Test matches
--> JC Laker (1) passed his previous highest score of 60 in first-class matches
--> SG Barnes (1) 50 in 136 balls, 129 minutes with 4 fours
--> DG Bradman (1) 50 in 111 balls, 100 minutes with 2 fours
--> DG Bradman (1) 100 in 233 balls, 211 minutes with 7 fours
--> DG Bradman (1) passed 1000 runs in first-class matches for the season when he reached 132
--> DG Bradman (1) passed 6500 runs in Test matches when he reached 12
--> AL Hassett (1) 50 in 197 balls, 183 minutes with 9 fours
--> AL Hassett (1) 100 in 333 balls, 308 minutes with 14 fours and 1 six
--> AL Hassett (1) passed 1000 runs in Test matches when he reached 118
--> RR Lindwall (1) passed 1000 runs in first-class matches when he reached 22
--> ERH Toshack (1) passed his previous highest score of 14 in first-class matches
--> L Hutton (2) 50 in 120 balls, 112 minutes with 9 fours
--> DCS Compton (2) 50 in 116 balls, 95 minutes with 5 fours
--> DCS Compton (2) 100 in 258 balls, 227 minutes with 12 fours
--> DCS Compton (2) 150 in 391 balls, 332 minutes with 15 fours
--> DCS Compton (2) passed 2000 runs in Test matches when he reached 117
--> TG Evans (2) passed 500 runs in Test matches when he reached 40
--> SG Barnes (2) 50 in 76 balls, 75 minutes with 9 fours
--> IWG Johnson made his debut in England in Test matches
--> RR Lindwall made his debut in England in Test matches
--> KR Miller made his debut in England in Test matches
--> D Tallon made his debut in England in Test matches
--> ERH Toshack made his debut in England in Test matches
--> AR Morris made his debut in England in Test matches
--> WA Johnston made his debut in England in Test matches
--> JC Laker made his debut in England in Test matches
--> WA Johnston achieved his best innings bowling analysis in Test matches when he dismissed AV Bedser in the England first innings (previous best was 4-44)
--> WA Johnston achieved his first five wickets in an innings in Test matches in the England first innings
--> AV Bedser reached 50 wickets in Test matches when he dismissed AL Hassett, his 2nd wicket in the Australia first innings

Scorecard Courtesy: www.cricketarchive.com

Lording it over England

"Rarely can a man have set out so certainly to command success." - John Arlott

A Team on a Mission

If anyone thought that after going one up in the series Bradman's lads would take it easy in the county matches that followed, they would be sorely disappointed. Two days after the first Test, the Australians took on a weak Northants side in what would be one of the easier matches on the tour. While the team could have taken it easy, for six-day-a-week cricket was not easy on the bodies, that's not how Bradman played his cricket. Instead, an innings victory followed and immediately thereafter it was on to Bramall Lane, Sheffield the 'Cutlery City', for a return match against formidable Yorkshire.

The Sheffield crowd were nicknamed the 'Grinders' and Jack Fingleton once said that they "believe once inside the ground they are part of the game". Bradman considered them a knowledgeable crowd and wrote: "the atmosphere was like a Test match but more intimate and concentrated." Most importantly, however, Yorkshire was Len Hutton's team and for Bradman, it was of paramount importance that all-out pressure was kept on Hutton by employing his main fast bowlers all hurling bouncers at England's premier batsman. In the end, however, the game became a bit too close for Bradman's comfort and he delayed his declaration making sure they could not lose the match even if it cost him a few fans.

The biggest takeaway for England from the first Test had been the realisation that they could not match the Australians for speed, to add to the woes of an ageing team and a lack of leadership. They made a few changes to the side for the second Test at Lord's, but the battle could only be won by their hardened veterans of whom only Dennis Compton had shown fight at Nottingham. Len Hutton, Cyril Washbrook, John Edrich, Norman Yardley, Godfrey Evans and Alec Bedser had to step up and be counted.

The Australians went in with an unchanged team despite some injury worries to Miller and Lindwall and the indifferent form of Bill Brown. Young Neil Harvey, who had been in magnificent form in the tour matches, would have to wait his turn to debut in England.

The Second Test at Lord's

The day the second Test started brought home to the teams the difference in how the two countries had fared economically in the Second World War. It was the day that Australia ended the rationing of meat and clothing, but the end of post-war austerity remained a faraway dream for England.

Lord's itself, despite being the home of the MCC, held different meanings for the two teams. The Australians had not won at 'Headquarters' until 1934, and then it would not lose a Test there into the 21st century. As Malcolm Knox wrote, "Lord's became Australia's favourite ground before it was England's, if it ever was. It is ironic though, that a ground and a club that preserved anachronistic class distinctions should have found its greatest fans and myth makers in Australia."

Bradman won the toss and batted first, not necessarily because he wanted first use of the pitch, but because it would give the spearhead of his bowling attack, Ray Lindwall some more time to recover from the injury. Lindwall had told Bradman in the morning: "Look Don, I'm absolutely sure I shall be all right. Leave me out on a form if you want to – but not on fitness." It would not take much to persuade Bradman. "All right, keep your hair on, you've talked me into it. We'll take the gamble."

Sidney Barnes strode out to open the innings with Morris. Barnes was desperate to get a big score. Displaying uncharacteristic anxiety he had asked for two hours of bowling from the ground staff before the other Australians arrived the day before the match. He had then told his teammates at dinner that he would make a hundred on this ground. For good measure, he had then put eight pounds on himself at 15 to 1 to score that century. In the second over from Coxton the medium pacer making his debut, Barnes gently pushed at a bad ball down the leg side straight into the hands of Len Hutton. He was out for a duck and Australia was 3 for 1.

Bradman walked in to huge applause. John Arlott described the first few balls: "Bradman made so stammering a start even for him, [such] that many spectators had to take a second look to be sure that it was indeed le maître. He almost played his first ball into his wicket, and immediately afterwards he was thumped upon the pad, and at the instant-roared appeal for lbw he looked up with the air of one who has enough troubles already without outsiders presuming to add to them."

He edged to gully, was dropped by Hutton in the leg trap with his score at 13, and with Morris managed to only record 32 in the first hour. "Arthur Morris and I were still there, but it could scarcely be said we were entirely responsible," is how he would later bluntly recollect that period of the match. He and Morris took the score to 87 before Bradman perished in the leg trap…for the third time in succession. Morris scored 105, an innings about which Bradman wrote: "Prior to the Lord's Test, Arthur had displayed good form under easy batting conditions, but had been in great difficulties when he encountered a turning wicket or a green-top … His batting visibly improved before our eyes. The measure of his superiority became more evident when a great batsman like Miller found the conditions beyond him while, at the same time, Morris was giving a superb display. Only the supreme combination of eyesight and natural genius could have done it. From that day onwards Arthur Morris was a far greater player than before." Then thanks largely to some gritty batting from Don Tallon, Australia's iconic wicketkeeper and the lower order, the innings closed at 350, a score they would scarcely have believed possible the previous day.

Keith **Miller**

Barnes, Miller and Bradman – The characters and exchanges that made it special

Ray Lindwall's groin was hurting when he started running in for his spell. Bradman's heart sank, but his assumption still was that he had Miller, despite Miller telling him before the innings that he didn't think his back would stand up to a new-ball spell. To make matters worse, as he stretched at slips for a Hutton catch off Lindwall, Miller felt his back give way. So when Bradman threw him the ball, Miller declined and just tossed it back to him. It was a gesture that would give rise to speculation for the rest of the tour about bad blood between Bradman who saw Miller as a bowler and bowled him to the ground in the interest of the team, and Miller who saw himself primarily as a batsman and resented the injuries that he was picking up from bowling so much.

This particular instance may, however, have been more innocent than it appeared if Miller's explanation is to be believed: "Now, there had been times before when I had had a bad back and bowled, and maybe [Bradman] thought this was another of those times. Then again he might have been plying a little psychology, thinking I would not have the temerity to refuse because of the huge crowd. Anyway, I simply could not bowl and I told him so and walked away. I was not playing the prima donna."

What this did, however, was put enormous pressure on Ray Lindwall, who was struggling with the groin injury but was determined that none of his colleagues should see his pain. John Arlott's description of Lindwall's bowling in that innings gives a rare insight into the determination and character of the bowler: "He was bowling beautifully, a lithe athlete that he is, his loose limbs ambling over the ground until the final four yards, when he gathered himself up and stretched taut every muscle." Lindwall would be instrumental in finally bowling out England for 215, only Dennis Compton once again providing resistance with a well-made 53.

When Barnes went out to bat the second time, the one thing that gave him comfort was that his eight pounds bet was still valid, and there was only one way to redeem himself – score that elusive century at Lord's. Psychologically he was a wreck. In a conversation that no modern batsman would ever have out in the middle, Barnes said to Godfrey Evans behind the stumps: "I've never felt so out of form, Godfrey. I hardly know which end of the bat to hold." Evans was to say later: "If ever a man looked set for a 'pair', he did."

But Barnes survived. In Jim Laker's first over Morris lobbed the ball back to Laker, who dropped it. In the same over Barnes stepped out, the ball spun away and Evans, one of the best keepers on the leg side in history, missed the stumping. Barnes told Evans: "Thanks Godfrey, that's the first bit of luck I've had in the last month. I hope I can take advantage of it."

At 122, Morris departed for 62 and Bradman came in.

Sid Barnes

Once again the leg trap came into play, but this time Bradman was ready for it and didn't give his wicket away. To give him some respite, Barnes now set, went on the offensive, scattering the field. In the process, Evan missed another stumping, one of five missed chances by the team as the pair went about batting England out of the match, Bradman now pulling with impunity.

Finally, after spending ten minutes at 96, Barnes straight drove Coxton for a four, running past Bradman's extended hand in delight then coming back to shake it. The 120 pounds was his and a century at Lord's was now written against his name on the Honours Board. He and Bradman then opened up before Barnes was finally out for 141.

In a dig at Barnes' pecuniary nature, Knox wrote in *Bradman's War*: "Typically, Barnes would sell 'the bat that made the century at Lord's on more than one occasion over the years. The actual one went to New South Wales' Ken Grieves."

Miller and Bradman then continued where Barnes had left off. Miller had become friendly with Princess Margaret and had been socialising with her at the Embassy Club and Kensington Palace. She had given him her royal standard, the flag given to her by the King on her 18th birthday. She was at the ground and Lord's was his second home from his time with the Air Force in England during the war. This time he could not disappoint and made sure he didn't, scoring 74 swashbuckling runs. Bradman departed for 89, and finally declared at 460 for 7 waiting until the pitch and run up area had dried enough after some rain, for his fast bowlers to bowl flat out. England was left to score an improbable 596 runs to win.

If the exchange between Bradman and Miller in the first innings had not ignited the rumours, the repeat in the second innings certainly did. After Lindwall's first over, Miller was thrown the ball, and just as in the first innings, Bradman found it back in his hand moments later. Barnes maintained that for good measure Miller curtly advised Bradman to have a go himself.

Back in the dressing room a conversation then allegedly took place that was later relayed back to Jack Fingleton. "I don't know what's up with you chaps, I'm 40 and I can do my full day's work in the field," said Bradman. Back came the reply from Miller: "So would I – if I had fibrositis during the war!"

Stunned silence accompanied this exchange because it was the first time anyone in the team had talked about Bradman's non-participation in the war and suspicions that his medical condition had been concocted to keep him out. An unfair accusation that would never quite go away notwithstanding all the evidence that pointed to Bradman's actual physical ailments. Speculation would forever be rife that the exchanges during this Test were the reason Miller would be dropped from the 1949-50 tour to South Africa when Bradman was a selector.

The Crushing Victory

Out on the field, the Englishmen faced up to some 'body music' from the Australian quicks. Washbrook showed enormous spirit taking hits on his body, but Hutton, already mentally shaky from his failings at the crease, was flinching and backing away from Lindwall. Even a lifelong fan of

Hutton's, Laurence Kitchin would describe his innings as "the most mysterious innings I've ever seen him play." It was a relief to one and all when Hutton departed for 13 edging Lindwall to slip. Washbrook departed to a remarkable catch by Tallon at ground level, a full toss yorker that took the bottom of the hand into his gloves, described by Bradman as "one of the most remarkable catches ever made behind the wicket." The English resistance crumbled and despite an unbeaten rearguard effort of 24 from Godfrey Evans, the inevitable was not long in coming. England was all out for 186 and Australia had won by 409 runs.

Fifteen minutes after the last wicket fell, heavy rain flooded Lord's. If this had been a non-Christian nation, the English could have blamed their Gods. For now, all of England could only agree that after only two Test matches the rampaging Australians were beginning to seem Invincible.

Scorecard - 2nd Test

England v Australia

Australia in British Isles 1948 (2nd Test)

Venue	Lord's Cricket Ground, St John's Wood on 24th, 25th, 26th, 28th, 29th June 1948 (5-day match)
Balls per over	6
Toss	Australia won the toss and decided to bat
Result	Australia won by 409 runs
Umpires	D Davies, CN Woolley
Close of play day 1	Australia (1) 258/7 (Tallon 25*, Lindwall 3*)
Close of play day 2	England (1) 207/9 (Bedser 6*, Wright 8*)
Close of play day 3	Australia (2) 343/4 (Miller 22*, Brown 7*)
Close of play day 4	England (2) 106/3 (Compton 29*, Dollery 21*)

Australia first innings		Runs	Balls	Mins	4s	6s
SG Barnes	c Hutton b Coxon	0				
AR Morris	c Hutton b Coxon	105		209	14	1
*DG Bradman	c Hutton b Bedser	38	104	115	-	

43

AL Hassett	b Yardley	47	175	-
KR Miller	lbw b Bedser	4		
WA Brown	lbw b Yardley	24	84	-
IWG Johnson	c Evans b Edrich	4		
+D Tallon	c Yardley b Bedser	53		
RR Lindwall	b Bedser	15		
WA Johnston	st Evans b Wright	29		
ERH Toshack	not out	20		
Extras	(3 b, 7 lb, 1 nb)			11
Total	(all out, 129.3 overs)			350

Fall of wickets:

1-3 (Barnes), 2-87 (Bradman), 3-166 (Morris), 4-173 (Miller), 5-216 (Hassett), 6-225 (Brown), 7-246 (Johnson), 8-275 (Lindwall), 9-320 (Tallon), 10-350 (Johnston, 129.3 ov)

England bowling	Overs	Mdns	Runs	Wkts	Wides		No-Balls
Bedser	43	14	100	4	-	-	
Coxon	35	10	90	2	-	-	
Edrich	8	0	43	1	-	-	
Wright	21.3	8	54	1	-		1
Laker	7	3	17	0	-	-	

| Yardley | 15 | 4 | 35 | 2 | - | - |

England first innings | | Runs | Balls | Mins | 4s | 6s

L Hutton	b Johnson	20				
C Washbrook	c Tallon b Lindwall	8				
WJ Edrich	b Lindwall	5		70	-	
DCS Compton	c Miller b Johnston	53				
HE Dollery	b Lindwall	0	2		-	-
*NWD Yardley	b Lindwall	44				
A Coxon	c and b Johnson	19				
+TG Evans	c Miller b Johnston	9				
JC Laker	c Tallon b Johnson	28				
AV Bedser	b Lindwall	9				
DVP Wright	not out	13				
Extras	(3 lb, 4 nb)					7
Total	(all out, 102.4 overs)					215

Fall of wickets:

1-17 (Washbrook), 2-32 (Hutton), 3-46 (Edrich), 4-46 (Dollery), 5-133 (Compton), 6-134 (Yardley), 7-145 (Evans), 8-186 (Laker), 9-197 (Coxon), 10-215 (Bedser, 102.4 ov)

Australia bowling	Overs	Mdns	Runs	Wkts	Wides	No-Balls
Lindwall	27.4	7	70	5	-	2
Johnston	22	4	43	2	-	2
Johnson	35	13	72	3	-	-
Toshack	18	11	23	0	-	-

Australia second innings		Runs	Balls	Mins	4s	6s
SG Barnes	c Washbrook b Yardley	141		277	14	2
AR Morris	b Wright	62				1
*DG Bradman	c Edrich b Bedser	89	162	185	13	-
AL Hassett	b Yardley	0	1	1	-	-
KR Miller	c Bedser b Laker	74				1
WA Brown	c Evans b Coxon	32				
RR Lindwall	st Evans b Laker	25				
IWG Johnson	not out	9				
+D Tallon	did not bat					
WA Johnston	did not bat					

ERH Toshack	did not bat	
Extras	(22 b, 5 lb, 1 nb)	28
Total	(7 wickets, declared, 130.2 overs)	460

Fall of wickets:

1-122 (Morris), 2-296 (Barnes), 3-296 (Hassett), 4-329 (Bradman), 5-416 (Brown), 6-445 (Miller), 7-460 (Lindwall, 130.2 ov)

England bowling	Overs	Mdns	Runs	Wkts	Wides	No-Balls
Bedser	34	6	112	1	-	-
Coxon	28	3	82	1	-	1
Edrich	2	0	11	0	-	-
Wright	19	4	69	1	-	-
Laker	31.2	6	111	2	-	-
Yardley	13	4	36	2	-	-
Compton	3	0	11	0	-	-

England second innings		Runs	Balls	Mins	4s	6s
L Hutton	c Johnson b Lindwall	13				
C Washbrook	c Tallon b Toshack	37				

WJ Edrich	c Johnson b Toshack	2			
DCS Compton	c Miller b Johnston	29			
HE Dollery	b Lindwall	37			
*NWD Yardley	b Toshack	11			
A Coxon	lbw b Toshack	0	2	-	-
+TG Evans	not out	24			
JC Laker	b Lindwall	0			
AV Bedser	c Hassett b Johnston	9			
DVP Wright	c Lindwall b Toshack	4			
Extras	(16 b, 4 lb)				20
Total	(all out, 78.1 overs)				186

Fall of wickets:

1-42 (Hutton), 2-52 (Edrich), 3-65 (Washbrook), 4-106 (Compton), 5-133 (Yardley), 6-133 (Coxon), 7-141 (Dollery), 8-141 (Laker), 9-158 (Bedser), 10-186 (Wright, 78.1 ov)

Australia bowling	Overs	Mdns	Runs	Wkts	Wides		No-Balls
Lindwall	23	9	61	3	-	-	
Johnston	33	15	62	2	-	-	
Toshack	20.1	6	40	5	-	-	
Johnson	2	1	3	0	-	-	

Notes

--> A Coxon made his debut in Test matches
--> WA Brown made his last appearance in Test matches
--> A Coxon made his last appearance in Test matches
--> WA Johnston (1) passed his previous highest score of 23 in Test matches
--> WA Johnston (1) passed his previous highest score of 24 in first-class matches
--> ERH Toshack (1) passed his previous highest score of 19 in Test matches
--> ERH Toshack (1) passed his previous highest score of 19 in first-class matches
--> SG Barnes (2) passed 1000 runs in Test matches when he reached 131
--> WA Brown (2) passed 1000 runs in first-class matches for the season when he reached 27
--> L Hutton (2) passed 2500 runs in Test matches when he reached 3
--> HE Dollery (2) passed his previous highest score of 17 in Test matches
--> HE Dollery (2) passed 1000 runs in first-class matches for the season when he reached 14
--> A Coxon made his debut for England in first-class matches
--> AV Bedser reached 350 wickets in first-class matches when he dismissed DG Bradman, his 1st wicket in the Australia first innings
--> RR Lindwall reached 150 wickets in first-class matches when he dismissed HE Dollery, his 2nd wicket in the England second innings

Scorecard Courtesy: www.cricketarchive.com

Bradman's 50th Test

As I ran up to bowl, Bradman seemed to know where the ball was going to pitch, what stroke he was going to play and how many runs he was going to score.

-- Jim Laker

In a Hurry in Surrey

In a scene that modern day players with their frequent complaints of the overload of cricket could not even begin to contemplate, the day after the Lord's Test match, the Australians found themselves in the field bowling to Surrey at The Oval. Granted, the travel had been minimal from St John's Wood to the southern suburbs of London, but the kind of rest the rigours of Test cricket demanded was clearly in short supply for the visitors.

However, not everyone was displeased. The likes of Sam Loxton who had been warming the changing room chairs for two Tests in a row were happy with the six days a week cricket and hurled it at the hapless Surrey batsmen on a war-damaged Oval pitch. Surrey was plainly lucky that Lindwall had been rested.

The exchanges between Keith Miller and Bradman continued to be frosty. Bradman was still peeved at Miller refusing to bowl in both innings of the Test citing an injury that his captain refused to believe existed. Miller had gone to a concert at the Royal Albert Hall after the Test, and when he staggered back into the Piccadilly at breakfast time, he bumped into his captain, who, later that morning, made him walk from fine leg to fine leg each over. A spectator very kindly offered Miller a bicycle. Bradman asked him to bowl, but after one over Miller again returned the ball to the skipper. He then failed with the bat and dropped two catches. The relationship was not getting any better.

Lindsay Hassett's fourth and Bradman's sixth century on the tour thus far gave the Aussies the lead and then McCool bowled out Surrey to leave the visitors 122 to win. Loxton asked Bradman if he could be sent up the order to get a knock, and Bradman, in a hurry to get to Wimbledon asked Loxton to open the batting with his mate young Neil Harvey, another man who had not yet played a Test on the tour. 20 overs later when the young pair jubilantly returned to the guy having knocked up the runs without too much trouble, an empty dressing room greeted them. The entire team had followed Bradman to Wimbledon to see Bromwich in the Wimbledon final against American Ralph Falkenburg. They had also taken all the cars.

When finally Loxton made it Centre Court on the Tube and sat down next to Doug Ring (Bradman was in the Royal Box) he turned to Loxton and asked: "Tell me, Sam. Did we win?"

The soon to be Invincibles would have to take their relaxation where they could get it, for right after the tennis, the team took the train to Bristol. The next day Gloucestershire awaited Bradman and his boys, an encounter the visitors would win by an innings and 363 runs.

The Controversial Dropping of Hutton

When the England team was announced for the third Test at Old Trafford, a stunned nation found the name of the greatest opening batsman in the world, and England's batting spearhead, Len Hutton, conspicuously missing.

Since the war, Len Hutton had averaged better than 40 against the Australians. No one other than Denis Compton

Len Hutton

had matched that. That summer, his two half-centuries for the

MCC and his 74 in the first Test at Nottingham had given England hope that he could anchor the top order. In the near darkness at Lord's in the second innings, he had been visibly uncomfortable, but the question was whether England was in any position to drop him on that basis.

To gauge how important he was to the English cause one only has to note the following exchange. Cyril Washbrook when asked by an Australian journalist who the best batsmen of the day in the world were, said: "Me and Len Hutton." "What about Bradman, Morris, Hassett and Barnes," the journalist asked? "They only have to face English bowling. Me and Len have to play Aussie bowling," came the answer.

And yet Hutton was not in the team. He had not even had the courtesy of being informed in person or on the phone – he heard the news on the radio. The selectors never explained their decision. About this lack of explanation, at the end of his career, Hutton would write: "Had they done so it might have softened the blow. Privately I held the selectors…to be wrong. That was all there was to it. Hard as I searched my mind for an answer, I came up with nothing, and I am still none the wiser."

There was widespread outrage across the country, and even the Aussies were taken aback. All kinds of conspiracy theories abounded including the close friendship between Bradman and one of the English selectors Robins which people said Bradman had used to influence the decision.

Morris would remark with a smile and a wink: "I wouldn't put it past Don. Maybe he was putting ideas in their heads." Neil Harvey would later say: "I believe Bradman would have tried to influence Robins. When you're playing an Ashes series, psychology comes into it. If a bloke looks out of form, you can try what you can to get rid of him. I can imagine Bradman voicing doubts about Hutton. I wasn't privy to it, but I wouldn't be at all surprised."

Be that as it may, when the teams gathered at Manchester for the third Test, there was no Hutton to open the batting for England. Psychologically, the Aussies were already ahead before a ball had been bowled.

Bradman's 50th Test

Since 1905, no Test match at Old Trafford had returned a result, the uncertain Manchester weather being the usual culprit. That didn't worry the Australians too much as they were already 2-0 ahead. Perhaps more significantly for them, the 50th test match of Don Bradman's career would be played at a ground where he conceded he had always been "notoriously unsuccessful."

Old Trafford was a ground that had suffered widespread damage from bombing during the war, with both the field and stadium being affected. While the ground was playable, parts of the stadium were unusable leaving limited seating. Such then was the setting when Don Bradman and Norman Yardley walked out for the toss.

Yardley won the toss and elected to bat on a cold and cloudy day. Bradman conceded he would have done the same. Cyril Washbrook faced the first ball of the innings in Hutton's absence (normally Washbrook would be at the non-striker's end while Hutton took first strike) accompanied by George Emmett making his Test debut. It would be the only Test Emmett would ever play for England.

At 28 for 2, Denis Compton walked in with all of England's hopes resting on his broad shoulders. Five runs later he had courted disaster as an attempt to hook a waist-high Lindwall bouncer resulted in the top edged ball smashing into his face splitting an eyebrow. Debutant Jack Crapp joined Edrich as the Englishmen gritted their teeth and proceeded to play themselves in. But at 119 for 5 Compton was forced to walk back in with his eyebrow stitched, joining captain Yardley at the crease.

Sam Loxton, finally in the Test side took out Yardley soon after. But first, in the company of Godfrey Evans and then Alec Bedser, Compton proceeded to play one of the greatest innings that had made him the hero of the post-war generation. When England was finally all out for 363 the next day, a day that John Arlott would describe as a day of "epic cricket for England," Compton was unbeaten on a defiant 145 garnered with the help of sixteen boundaries in his five-and-a-half hours stay at the crease. Speaking to me about this innings and others that Dennis Compton played in that immediate post-war period, David Frith would recount how "[Dennis] Compton grabbed the imagination of all, us young boys."

With Sid Barnes injured while building, Ian Johnson was sent in with Arthur Morris to open the Australian innings. But with Johnson departing quickly and Bradman's "notoriously unsuccessful" run at Old Trafford continuing,

Australia was soon 13 for 2. Morris and Keith Miller rebuilt the innings but Barnes, despite collapsing from chest pain was forced to come in the next day at 139 for 5, only to be carried back to the hospital a run later from the pain. Australia managed to avoid the follow-on but when the innings ended at 221, England, for the first time in the series was ahead by 142 runs.

Australian backs to the wall

When England walked in for the second innings they were in no doubt about what was about to happen. Washbrook would say later: "We had to remember that this was the first time in a post-war Test that the Australians had been in trouble. Their intentions to hit back with all possible means in their power could not be doubted." And so it played out.

With their backs to the wall, the Aussie aggression re-emerged in all its wonderful glory. Keith Miller's back had a miraculous recovery (or so it seemed to the Englishmen) and in company with Lindwall, a barrage of short-pitched bowling started and it would continue. Edrich and Washbrook took the fight to the Aussies, employing the hook with magnificent effect. Talking about his hooks off Lindwall just off his nose, Bill Edrich would say: "The best way is to let it come here (pointing to a spot between his eyes), then you've got to hit it. The hook's safe enough as long as you remember that the ball never hurts as much as you think it's going to." Keith Miller, not one to part with compliments easily, called Edrich a "deadly hooker."

Putting together a 124-run partnership the two helped England pile up a substantial lead and England ended the third day at 174 for 3. The fourth day was washed out by rain and when Yardley declared at the same score on the fifth morning, Australia was left to score 317 for a victory, by no means an unachievable task, but a difficult one that would give England the chance to go for a victory by picking up wickets quickly.

As it would happen however the rain persisted so that the entire morning session's play was lost. Bradman asked his batsmen to down the shutters, no doubt with invincibility on his mind, and when stumps was called, the visitors had made 92 for 1 in the 61 overs that were bowled.

Bradman's boys may not have been 3-0 up, but by escaping unscathed from Old Trafford, they had taken another huge step towards Invincibility.

Scorecard - 3rd Test

England v Australia

	Australia in British Isles 1948 (3rd Test)
Venue	Old Trafford, Manchester on 8th, 9th, 10th, 12th, 13th July 1948 (5-day match)
Balls per over	6
Toss	England won the toss and decided to bat
Result	Match drawn
Umpires	F Chester, D Davies
Close of play day 1	England (1) 231/7 (Compton 64*, Bedser 4*)
Close of play day 2	Australia (1) 126/3 (Morris 48*, Miller 23*)
Close of play day 3	England (2) 174/3 (Washbrook 85*, Crapp 19*)
Close of play day 4	No play

England first innings

		Runs	Balls	Mins	4s	6s
C Washbrook	b Johnston	11		30	1	-
GM Emmett	c Barnes b Lindwall	10		47	-	-
WJ Edrich	c Tallon b Lindwall	32		170	5	-

DCS Compton	not out	145	324	16	-
JF Crapp	lbw b Lindwall	37	115	4	1
HE Dollery	b Johnston	1	5	-	-
*NWD Yardley	c Johnson b Toshack	22	83	3	-
+TG Evans	c Johnston b Lindwall	34	76	4	-
AV Bedser	run out	37	145	7	-
R Pollard	b Toshack	3	26	-	-
JA Young	c Bradman b Johnston	4	10	-	-
Extras	(7 b, 17 lb, 3 nb)				27
Total	(all out, 171.5 overs)				363

Fall of wickets:

1-22 (Washbrook), 2-28 (Emmett), 3-96 (Crapp), 4-97 (Dollery), 5-119 (Edrich), 6-141 (Yardley), 7-216 (Evans), 8-337 (Bedser), 9-352 (Pollard), 10-363 (Young, 171.5 ov)

Australia bowling	Overs	Mdns	Runs	Wkts	Wides	No-Balls
Lindwall	40	8	99	4	-	3
Johnston	45.5	13	67	3	-	-
Loxton	7	0	18	0	-	-
Toshack	41	20	75	2	-	-
Johnson	38	16	77	0	-	-

Australia first innings		Runs	Balls	Mins	4s	6s
AR Morris	c Compton b Bedser	51		218	6	-
IWG Johnson	c Evans b Bedser	1		7	-	-
*DG Bradman	lbw b Pollard	7	7	9	1	-
AL Hassett	c Washbrook b Young	38		101	5	-
KR Miller	lbw b Pollard	31		75	4	-
SG Barnes	retired hurt	1		25	-	-
SJE Loxton	b Pollard	36		77	6	-
+D Tallon	c Evans b Edrich	18		30	1	-
RR Lindwall	c Washbrook b Bedser	23		106	3	-
WA Johnston	c Crapp b Bedser	3		13	-	-
ERH Toshack	not out	0		1	-	-
Extras	(5 b, 4 lb, 3 nb)					12
Total	(all out, 93 overs)					221

Fall of wickets:

1-3 (Johnson), 2-13 (Bradman), 3-82 (Hassett), 4-135 (Miller), 5-139 (Morris), 6-172 (Tallon), 7-208 (Loxton), 8-219 (Johnston), 9-221 (Lindwall, 93 ov)

England bowling	Overs	Mdns	Runs	Wkts	Wides	No-Balls
Bedser	36	12	81	4	-	2
Pollard	32	9	53	3	-	1
Edrich	7	3	27	1	-	-
Yardley	4	0	12	0	-	-
Young	14	5	36	1	-	-

England second innings		Runs	Balls	Mins	4s	6s
C Washbrook	not out	85		208	11	-
GM Emmett	c Tallon b Lindwall	0		3	-	-
WJ Edrich	run out	53		138	8	1
DCS Compton	c Miller b Toshack	0		6	-	-
JF Crapp	not out	19		55	2	-
HE Dollery	did not bat					
*NWD Yardley	did not bat					
+TG Evans	did not bat					
AV Bedser	did not bat					
R Pollard	did not bat					
JA Young	did not bat					

Extras   (9 b, 7 lb, 1 w)   17

Total   (3 wickets, declared, 69 overs)   174

Fall of wickets:

1-1 (Emmett), 2-125 (Edrich), 3-129 (Compton)

Australia bowling	Overs	Mdns	Runs	Wkts	Wides	No-Balls
Lindwall	14	4	37	1	-	-
Miller	14	7	15	0	1	-
Johnston	14	3	34	0	-	-
Loxton	8	2	29	0	-	-
Toshack	12	5	26	1	-	-
Johnson	7	3	16	0	-	-

Australia second innings		Runs	Balls	Mins	4s	6s
AR Morris	not out	54		156	9	-
IWG Johnson	c Crapp b Young	6		32	1	-
*DG Bradman	not out	30	146	122	6	-
AL Hassett	did not bat					
KR Miller	did not bat					

SG Barnes	did not bat	
SJE Loxton	did not bat	
+D Tallon	did not bat	
RR Lindwall	did not bat	
WA Johnston	did not bat	
ERH Toshack	did not bat	
Extras	(2 nb)	2
Total	(1 wicket, 61 overs)	92

Fall of wickets:

1-10 (Johnson)

England bowling	Overs	Mdns	Runs	Wkts	Wides	No-Balls
Bedser	19	12	27	0	-	1
Pollard	10	8	6	0	-	-
Young	21	12	31	1	-	-
Compton	9	3	18	0	-	1
Edrich	2	0	8	0	-	-

Notes

--> GM Emmett made his debut in Test matches
--> JF Crapp made his debut in Test matches
--> GM Emmett made his last appearance in Test matches
--> DCS Compton (1) passed 18000 runs in first-class matches when he reached 86
--> AV Bedser (1) passed his previous highest score of 30 in Test matches
--> R Pollard (1) passed 3000 runs in first-class matches when he reached 3
--> SJE Loxton (1) passed 1500 runs in first-class matches when he reached 28
--> C Washbrook (2) passed 1000 runs in Test matches when he reached 13
--> AR Morris (2) passed 1000 runs in Test matches when he reached 30
--> GM Emmett made his debut for England in first-class matches
--> SJE Loxton made his debut in England in Test matches
--> RR Lindwall reached 50 wickets in Test matches when he dismissed WJ Edrich, his 3rd wicket in the England first innings
--> DCS Compton retired hurt in the England first innings having scored 4 (team score 33/2) - he returned when the score was 119/5
--> SG Barnes retired hurt in the Australia first innings having scored 1 (team score 139/5)

Scorecard Courtesy: www.cricketarchive.com

The Greatest Test Match

"I know I shall never cherish any memory more than the reception at Leeds at the Test here. Not only was it the greatest I have ever received in this country, but the greatest I have ever received from any public anywhere in the world." - Don Bradman, 1948

Playing to Bradman's Plan

When the 1948 tour started, while Invincibility was an early objective, it was not the primary one, nor the secondary. This was the golden age of the Ashes contest, and Australia had had the urn securely locked up since 1934. The last time they had given it away to England was during the 1932-33 Bodyline series and a year later with neither Larwood nor Jardine in the team, they had wrested it right back from the lion's den. In 1948, Bradman's first priority had been to retain the Ashes. This done, a win or draw in the fourth Test at Leeds would clinch the series. Invincibility, the third goal, he was convinced, would follow.

The Ashes retained, before the team moved on to Leeds, it was time to let down the hair. Miller and Lindwall, inseparable on the field and off it, were determined to enjoy the time off before the match against county champions Middlesex at Lord's. And so they did.

Bradman found them in a dishevelled state the morning of the Middlesex match. Miller was in any case not a morning person and rarely arrived at a ground more than 15 minutes before the start of a match. But in this instance, Lindwall and Miller had taken their 'relaxation' a bit too seriously. Lindwall asked to be excused from the match, but Bradman would have none of it. Sixteen fruitless overs later, Lindwall lay on the grass exhausted. Bradman walked over to him and quipped: "Have a nice time last night, Ray?"

The march towards invincibility was far from over, and Bradman would not let anyone forget it.

The Greatest Test – Leeds 1948

Not surprisingly, when the teams arrived in Leeds, Len Hutton was back in the side after being inexplicably dropped from the team at Lord's. There were only two Tests left, and even if it was already known that the urn would remain in Australia, England's series could yet be salvaged by wresting victories in the remaining matches. Laker joined the team to beef up the bowling.

For Australia, the injury to Barnes meant that after waiting for more than half the tour, playing every tour match that he could, young Neil Harvey would finally make his Ashes debut. In fact, Harvey thought Bill Brown would come in to replace Barnes and was content to be the twelfth man again as he had been for the first three Tests. He was having breakfast the morning of the match when Bradman came and sat down next to him. "You're playing today" was all he said before walking out of the dining room.

Neil Harvey - a worthy successor

As Malcolm Knox put it, "Bringing in the teenager was a bold move by Bradman. Brown, the champion opener of the 1930s had been the outstanding batsman of the non-Test games, with four centuries and a double century....Yet, Bradman was able to cast his pragmatism aside and yield to his imagination. The boy would play." The decision would prove crucial and launch the teenaged Neil Harvey, who had already scored a magnificent 153 against India the previous Australian summer, as the worthy successor to Bradman and the mainstay of the Australian batting as well as its leader for much of the next decade and a half.

For Bradman himself, Leeds was a happy hunting ground and the memories of his 334 in 1930, 304 in 1934 and a brilliant 103 in 1938 against an unplayable Hedley Verity were fresh in the memories of fans overflowing the stands. Headingley was surely Bradman's home away from home. The fans thronging the ground that July day of 1948 wanted only two things – a fitting farewell innings from Bradman, followed by an English victory.

A letter written by a fan during the second evening of the Test match that Bradman was to receive a few days after the Leeds Test concluded is a measure of the adoration and esteem in which he was held by English fans who knew he was a once-in-a-lifetime phenomenon and treated him as one of their own. The letter read:

"Dear Mr. Bradman,

My friends and I gambled on our English weather, three doubtful cycles and the fortune of the road, and cycled to Leeds to see the second day of the Test. My friend broke a gear on the way back, I broke a mudguard and we both had to push our exhausted friend over the moors, but it was well worth it.

Yours very sincerely

From one hopeful cricketer,

One not so hopeful,

And

One who cannot play at all."

A Dream Start for England

Yardley won the toss and Len Hutton walked out to bat to a thunderous ovation. Hutton may have been away for just a game, but the Yorkshire crowd were making sure the selectors received the message about what they thought of the ill-conceived decision to drop him the previous Test.

Tiger O'Reilly commented that the wicket was "so green that it was difficult to decide where the out-field ended and the pitch began. But any thoughts the Aussies had had about a quick breakthrough were soon dispelled.

Hutton drove Miller magnificently through the off side in his first over, and so brutal was he that an off-colour Miller was replaced after two overs. Lindwall was struggling from the other end to make an impact. John Arlott spoke in wonder: "never in the series had England's first wicket outlasted the spell of the opening bowlers."

Even when Toshack and Johnston had a go, they could not get a breakthrough. After lunch it got worse as the openers attacked, taking five fours off Lindwall. As the century stand came up in 131 minutes, Arlott referred to the stand as being "behind the clock, but ahead of expectation – even abreast of hope." As the batting grew more masterful, the bowling appeared ragged. Jack Fingleton called it "atrociously bad." Finally, Hutton batting at 81, played a forward defensive stroke to Lindwall and somehow missed the ball which knocked back his stumps. The pair had put on 168, by far the highest opening partnership for England in the series.

Washbrook steadfastly refused to indulge in the hook shot which had been his downfall more than once and completed his century, finally dismissed for 143. John Edrich and Alec Bedser carried on the unrelenting carnage on the Australian bowlers and when both departed, England was 426 for 4. The rest of the batsmen could put on only 70 runs more and England was all out for 496 in the final session of the second day. The wrecker in chief was Sam Loxton, picking up his first three wickets in Test cricket and wrapping up the tail.

Bradman and Hassett took the visitors to 63 for 1 at stumps after losing Morris early.

The Emergence of a Worthy Successor

If Australia was to take the fight to the hosts, the start on the third day was going to be crucial. With Don Bradman and Lindsay Hassett at the crease, there was no reason to believe otherwise. A stunning over from medium pacer Dick Pollard changed all that. He first got Hassett to edge one to slip, and when Miller responded to Bradman's serious words of caution by smashing the first ball for three, Pollard bowled one on Bradman's middle stump that kept very low and knocked back his off. Suddenly Australia was 68 for 3 and in serious trouble.

Bradman later recalled his thoughts as he passed Harvey on his way back to the pavilion: "A silent prayer from me went with him. Surely it was asking too much of him to succeed where we had failed."

Neil Harvey, on the other hand, exhibited none of the nervousness the others around him seemed to feel. He had promised himself he would only use one of the new unmarked bats he had been presented in England by Slazenger who sponsored Bradman's bats, if he went in to bat in a Test match. So holding a brand new bat under his arm that hadn't even been touched by a practice ball, jauntily cap less, Harvey walked up to take guard. That done he met Keith Miller mid-pitch. Miller, just about to give the young man some words of encouragement, was taken aback when Harvey spoke first and said: "What's going on here, eh? Let's get into them!"

Neil Harvey had arrived on the big stage and planned to stay there for a long time.

The next hour was one about which Arlott was to write later: "I don't think I have known a more enjoyable hour of cricket." Miller was in his elements, one of his sixes claiming a victim in a young blonde in a green dress who had to be removed in an ambulance, and inspired by his belligerence, Harvey let loose as well. The two Victorians had taken the fight to the hosts. Tiger O'Reilly penned: "They laid about them with such joyful abandon, that it would have been difficult, if not absolutely impossible, to gather from their methods of going about it that they were actually retrieving a tremendously difficult situation."

When Miller was finally out to an extraordinary catch by Edrich at short fine leg for 58, all of England breathed a sigh of relief. But Harvey was only getting started. As a nervous Sam Loxton walked in, Harvey walked up to his closest mate and told him confidently: "They can't bowl,

Sammy." He then went back to take strike and proceeded to loosen up with strokes all around the wicket, particularly severe in cutting virtually anything pitched outside the off. At lunch, Australia was 204 for 4, a remarkable recovery.

After lunch, Loxton joined the party with the advent of the new ball. He hit Pollard for successive fours and then a six. Godfrey Evans behind the stumps told him: "It wouldn't have been a six at Melbourne." Pat came the reply: We are not in Melbourne and I was easing up on the shot."

The pair slowed down as Harvey reached 99 and stayed there for the better part of three overs. On ABC Radio in Australia, Alan McGilvray, the voice of cricket in Australia at the time, said: "Don't worry, Mr and Mrs Harvey, he'll get them." And so he did, off driving Laker for a single, bringing up his century in 177 minutes. Harvey would recall: "I can still feel Laker pat me on the shoulder. I felt like I had won the lottery."

With youthful exuberance, Harvey went berserk, hitting Laker for three fours in a row over midwicket and perishing in his attempt to hit the fourth, bowled, missing the ball on the cross-batted stroke. He had scored 112. "I was young and stupid," Harvey would admit with a wry smile, years later. With Australia still 200 behind, Harvey expected to be roasted on his return to the hut, but Bradman just said: "Well played." In his autobiography Farewell to Cricket, Bradman would explain his restraint, writing that the dismissal "was a natural end to one of the greatest innings any batsman, old or young, has ever played."

In the 1970s, when Bradman, Loxton and Harvey were national selectors, Loxton would take that bat which Harvey had never used again for Bradman to sign on. Harvey, the only surviving member of the Invincibles side, still has the bat on which an inscription in fountain pen reads: "This bat is a symbol of a great innings by my friend Neil Harvey in Australia's greatest ever Test victory, Leeds, 1948. Don Bradman."

Neil Harvey would go on to play 79 Tests for Australia by the time he retired in 1963, scoring 6149 runs at an average of 48.41 with the help of 21 centuries. His first class career would net him 20,000 runs.

Setting up the greatest chase in the history of Test cricket

The Australian batting in the innings now resembled a relay team – Miller had given way to Harvey's assault, and now it was Loxton's turn. He started with a six to reach his 50. He followed it with four more. At 93, he perished trying to "hit a seven" in the words of his teammate Morris. By then the damage to the morale of the English bowlers was non-reversible. Lindwall would pile on the misery, Lindwall making 76 with Australia's final score on the fourth morning reading 458. But with the pitch wearing, England rather fancied their chances of a win.

Hutton and Washbrook started where they had left off in the first innings, registering a world record as the first Test openers to register two century partnerships in a match for the second time. When they were out, Edrich and Compton took over. One of John Arlott's most evocative quips came at this stage as he described Compton cutting Lindwall "so late that his stroke was within a sparrow's blink of being posthumous." With Evans chipping in as well, when Yardley declared the next morning, Australia was left 404 to score in 344 minutes.

It was an interesting situation. Not only had no team ever scored more than 350 runs to win in the fourth innings of a Test match in the 72-years of Test cricket, no side had won a Test against a declaration in 70-years. A draw was the least likely scenario given the forces at play. Either Bradman's dream would take a huge step forward this day or it would lie irrevocably shattered.

The previous night Bradman had written in his diary: "We are set 400 to win and I fear we may be defeated." In the morning, he gathered his team around him in the dressing room and paraphrased the word another Australian, Fred Spofforth had uttered when the first Ashes had been won. Bradman said: "Come on boys, we can win this match, we can do it."

Best friends Sam Loxton and Neil Harvey 1948

The Greatest Chase

Waiting for the start, Morris read the headlines of the British press that morning that predicted Australia would be all out by lunch. That strengthened their resolve, already bolstered by Bradman's stirring speech.

Hassett and Morris started slowly, and when Laker came on, it was clear the ball was turning square on this final day pitch. Uncharacteristically, Evans missed two stumpings that morning, but eventually, Hassett departed to Compton's occasional Chinaman bowling. Bradman walked into a reception he would write about later as "the greatest I have ever received from any public anywhere in the world." He had not had a great series by his own exalted standards, but this was the kind of big occasion that Bradman truly thrived in.

But this was not going to be easy. A Laker delivery pitched outside off and went past Bradman's leg stump. Then in a single over from Compton, he failed to spot a Chinaman's googly and edged past slip, then was dropped by Crapp in the slips doing exactly the same, and the last ball of the overwrapped him on the pads, just above stump height. But with Compton only a part-time bowler, and no wrist spinner to support Laker on a turning pitch, Yardley was running out of options. In desperation, he threw the ball to Hutton, a reluctant leg spinner at the best of times.

Bradman and Morris launched into Hutton in a display of savagery that Headingley had not seen in many a year, a spell that would be referred to a distraught radio listener as "those martyred overs". By lunch, the Australians were 121 for 1 and the crowd had started making their unhappiness felt.

After lunch Compton replaced Hutton and Morris went after him, shielding the uncomfortable Bradman. At the score of 59 Yardley dropped Bradman and Evans missed another stumping off Laker. England was quickly unravelling. A total of eight chances were missed by England in that innings. A feeling of hopelessness swept through the team.

At 3.10pm Australia was halfway home at 200, and at 4 pm they were 250. Morris and Bradman had both reached their centuries. At tea, Australia needed 112 runs in 105 minutes. By 5 pm the crowd had forgotten that the first four days of the Test had belonged to England.

At 615pm, fifteen minutes before stumps, Neil Harvey flicked a ball off his legs for 4 and Australia had completed the greatest chase in Test cricket and won the series.

It was entirely appropriate that the future and present of Australian cricket were together at the crease when the win came. Harvey would, however, lament years later: "It was my fault he didn't average a hundred in Tests! I hit the four."

But that is a story to look forward to. For now, only the last goal remained – **Invincibility** was within striking distance.

Scorecard - 4th Test

England v Australia

Australia in British Isles 1948 (4th Test)

Venue	Headingley, Leeds on 22nd, 23rd, 24th, 26th, 27th July 1948 (5-day match)
Balls per over	6
Toss	England won the toss and decided to bat
Result	Australia won by 7 wickets
Umpires	HG Baldwin, F Chester
Close of play day 1	England (1) 268/2 (Edrich 41*, Bedser 0*)
Close of play day 2	Australia (1) 63/1 (Hassett 13*, Bradman 31*)
Close of play day 3	Australia (1) 457/9 (Lindwall 76*, Toshack 12*)
Close of play day 4	England (2) 362/8 (Evans 47*, Laker 14*)

England first innings		Runs	Balls	Mins	4s	6s
L Hutton	b Lindwall	81		187		-
C Washbrook	c Lindwall b Johnston	143		317	22	-
WJ Edrich	c Morris b Johnson	111		314	13	1
AV Bedser	c and b Johnson	79		177	8	2

DCS Compton	c Saggers b Lindwall	23	55	-
JF Crapp	b Toshack	5		
*NWD Yardley	b Miller	25		
K Cranston	b Loxton	10		
+TG Evans	c Hassett b Loxton	3		
JC Laker	c Saggers b Loxton	4		
R Pollard	not out	0		
Extras	(2 b, 8 lb, 1 nb, 1 w)		12	
Total	(all out, 192.1 overs)		496	

Fall of wickets:

1-168 (Hutton), 2-268 (Washbrook), 3-423 (Bedser), 4-426 (Edrich), 5-447 (Crapp), 6-473 (Compton), 7-486 (Cranston), 8-490 (Evans), 9-496 (Laker), 10-496 (Yardley, 192.1 ov)

Australia bowling	Overs	Mdns	Runs	Wkts	Wides	No-Balls
Lindwall	38	10	79	2	-	-
Miller	17.1	2	43	1	-	-
Johnston	38	12	86	1	1	1
Toshack	35	6	112	1	-	-
Loxton	26	4	55	3	-	-
Johnson	33	9	89	2	-	-
Morris	5	0	20	0	-	-

Australia first innings		Runs	Balls	Mins	4s	6s
AR Morris	c Cranston b Bedser	6				
AL Hassett	c Crapp b Pollard	13				
*DG Bradman	b Pollard	33	56	59	-	
KR Miller	c Edrich b Yardley	58				2
RN Harvey	b Laker	112		188	17	-
SJE Loxton	b Yardley	93		135	8	5
IWG Johnson	c Cranston b Laker	10				
RR Lindwall	c Crapp b Bedser	77				
+RA Saggers	st Evans b Laker	5				
WA Johnston	c Edrich b Bedser	13				
ERH Toshack	not out	12				
Extras	(9 b, 14 lb, 3 nb)					26
Total	(all out, 136.2 overs)					458

Fall of wickets:

1-13 (Morris), 2-65 (Hassett), 3-68 (Bradman), 4-189 (Miller), 5-294 (Harvey), 6-329 (Johnson), 7-344 (Loxton), 8-355 (Saggers), 9-403 (Johnston), 10-458 (Lindwall, 136.2 ov)

England bowling	Overs	Mdns	Runs	Wkts	Wides		No-Balls
Bedser	31.2	4	92	3	-		2
Pollard	38	6	104	2	-		1
Cranston	14	1	51	0	-	-	
Edrich	3	0	19	0	-	-	
Laker	30	8	113	3	-	-	
Yardley	17	6	38	2	-	-	
Compton	3	0	15	0	-	-	

England second innings		Runs	Balls	Mins	4s	6s
L Hutton	c Bradman b Johnson	57			1	
C Washbrook	c Harvey b Johnston	65			1	
WJ Edrich	lbw b Lindwall	54			1	
DCS Compton	c Miller b Johnston	66				
JF Crapp	b Lindwall	18				
*NWD Yardley	c Harvey b Johnston	7				
K Cranston	c Saggers b Johnston	0	2		-	-
+TG Evans	not out	47				
AV Bedser	c Hassett b Miller	17			4	-

JC Laker	not out	15
R Pollard	did not bat	
Extras	(4 b, 12 lb, 3 nb)	19
Total	(8 wickets, declared, 107 overs)	365

Fall of wickets:

1-129 (Washbrook), 2-129 (Hutton), 3-232 (Edrich), 4-260 (Crapp), 5-277 (Yardley), 6-278 (Cranston), 7-293 (Compton), 8-330 (Bedser)

Australia bowling	Overs	Mdns	Runs	Wkts	Wides	No-Balls
Lindwall	26	6	84	2	-	-
Miller	21	5	53	1	-	-
Johnston	29	5	95	4	-	3
Loxton	10	2	29	0	-	-
Johnson	21	2	85	1	-	-

Australia second innings		Runs	Balls	Mins	4s	6s
AR Morris	c Pollard b Yardley	182		291	33	-

AL Hassett	c and b Compton	17		74	1	-
*DG Bradman	not out	173	292	255	29	-
KR Miller	lbw b Cranston	12		30	2	-
RN Harvey	not out	4			1	-
SJE Loxton	did not bat					
IWG Johnson	did not bat					
RR Lindwall	did not bat					
+RA Saggers	did not bat					
WA Johnston	did not bat					
ERH Toshack	did not bat					
Extras	(6 b, 9 lb, 1 nb)					16
Total	(3 wickets, 114.1 overs)					404

Fall of wickets:

1-57 (Hassett), 2-358 (Morris), 3-396 (Miller)

England bowling	Overs	Mdns	Runs	Wkts	Wides		No-Balls
Bedser	21	2	56	0	-		1
Pollard	22	6	55	0	-	-	
Laker	32	11	93	0	-	-	

Compton	15	3	82	1	-	-
Hutton	4	1	30	0	-	-
Yardley	13	1	44	1	-	-
Cranston	7.1	0	28	1	-	-

Notes

--> RA Saggers made his debut in Test matches
--> K Cranston made his last appearance in Test matches
--> R Pollard made his last appearance in Test matches
--> ERH Toshack made his last appearance in Test matches
--> C Washbrook (1) passed his previous highest score of 112 in Test matches
--> WJ Edrich (1) passed 1500 runs in Test matches when he reached 14
--> WJ Edrich (1) passed 17500 runs in first-class matches when he reached 91
--> AV Bedser (1) passed his previous highest score of 37 in Test matches
--> SJE Loxton (1) passed his previous highest score of 80 in Test matches
--> AR Morris (2) passed his previous highest score of 155 in Test matches
--> AR Morris (2) passed 4000 runs in first-class matches when he reached 171
--> DG Bradman (2) passed 27000 runs in first-class matches when he reached 100
--> RA Saggers made his debut for Australia in first-class matches
--> RN Harvey made his debut in England in Test matches
--> SJE Loxton achieved his best innings bowling analysis in Test matches when he dismissed JC Laker in the England first innings (previous best was 2-61)
--> ERH Toshack reached 50 wickets in first-class matches for the season when he dismissed JF Crapp, his 1st wicket in the England first innings
--> IWG Johnson reached 200 wickets in first-class matches when he dismissed AV Bedser, his 1st wicket in the England first innings
--> RR Lindwall reached 50 wickets in first-class matches for the season when he dismissed JF Crapp, his 2nd wicket in the England second innings

Scorecard Courtesy: www.cricketarchive.com

Forever Invincibles

"We didn't start off with any particular thought of going undefeated, but it evolved in Don's mind when we started to win matches." – Bill Brown on being an Invincible

Unfinished Work, Punishing Schedule

The series had been won, the miracle at Headingley achieved, and yet for Bradman the foot could not be taken off the gas pedal, for invincibility was still some distance away.

He was more aware than anyone else that ten years ago in 1938, his team had been undefeated until that point, but had been unable to remain so. Warwick Armstrong's all-conquering team of 1921 had sustained their drive to invincibility until the last week of the tour when an Argentinian bowler Clem Gibson, part of a ragged team of retired Test and county players under the captaincy of retired English captain Archie MacLaren had almost single-handedly wrought destruction upon the mighty Australians. As Malcolm Knox put it aptly in Bradman's War, "Bradman was now competing with history."

In yet another reflection of how much tighter schedules were and the far more challenging environment players of the time faced compared to the relaxed lives of their counterparts of today, the morning after the Leeds Test the Australians had an encounter with Derbyshire, four hours away by train. Morris and Johnson were given leave to go and watch the Olympic Games in London, but Bradman led a strong team into the stadium the next morning at Derby, only a few hours after they had checked into their hotel past midnight.

Winning the toss and batting first, Brown allowed his mates to get a bit of a shut-eye as he led from the front with a century. Bradman, Miller, Loxton added half centuries. With 456 on the board, Derbyshire was dismissed for 240 and asked to follow on. In the second innings, Colin McCool, an early precursor of the Shane Warne style of bowling, sent down his expansively flighted leg breaks and deceptive googlies to take 6 for 77 and precipitated a Derby collapse for 182, handing the visitors victory by an innings and 34 runs.

Once again the visitors embarked on a train journey, this time taking five hours in order to take on county championship leaders Glamorgan the next morning at Swansea in Wales. In a rain-affected match where Bradman himself took a much-deserved break, the county managed a draw against the visitors. Another four hour journey up north to Birmingham and it was time to face Warwickshire the following morning, where for the first time (but memorably not the last) the Australians would face the leg spin of 36-year old Eric Hollies.

All summer England had struggled with its spin bowling, with Laker only enjoying limited success, and the late Hedley Verity's absence was felt every time the Australians went out to bat. But it was left to the fag end of the tour before a genuine match winner like Hollies would be unleashed on the Australians. In this instance, the fault lay less with the selectors and more at the door of the man himself. Hollies did not like to travel, and between 1935 and 1947 he didn't play a Test match despite match-winning performances like ten wickets in an innings against Nottinghamshire in 1946. Jack Fingleton was to report that he was informed Hollies liked Test cricket even less than he liked to travel.

In 1948, bowling against Bradman's boys, Hollies could not prevent the Australians from winning the match against his county by nine wickets, but his 8 for 107 in the first innings, the best bowling figures by an Englishman on the 1948 tour, would have an impact well beyond the numbers themselves or indeed the result of this tour match.

Hollies first dismissed Brown and Morris. Bradman by then had scored 31 but was having trouble reading Hollies even with the years of experience he had had against the great Clarrie Grimmett. Hollies bowled him with a flighted googly and got past Neil Harvey's defence the very next ball. By the time he took Hassett, his dismissal of the entire top order had booked him a ticket to the final Test at the Oval. It would turn out to be a historic decision by the English selectors.

The Final Test – Oval 1948

While the weather had largely held up with brief interruptions to the tour matches, the few days leading up to the final Test at the Kennington Oval saw incessant unseasonal rains that lashed the length and breadth of England. London was not spared. In the days of uncovered pitches, the perfect batting surface at the Kennington Oval that had greeted Bradman for much of his career was nowhere in evidence when the teams arrived at the ground.

It was not an auspicious start, for not only was this Don Bradman's farewell Test match, but invincibility beckoned beyond the Surrey clouds, and she was not a forgiving mistress.

The wet wicket meant changes to the team had to be made. Ian Johnson was replaced by the now fit Sidney Barnes to strengthen the batting. Toshack who was injured was replaced by leg spinner Ring for his first Test, and Don Tallon, one of the greatest of Australian wicketkeepers came back from injury. With more rain on the cards, on an overcast afternoon, Norman Yardley chose to bat first on winning the toss. He thought the pitch might be wet enough to hamper the bowlers more than the batsmen. Bradman admitted later that like at Nottingham, he was happy to lose the toss and have the decision taken out of his hands.

Less than an hour after the delayed start, Yardley's decision was already being questioned. With Keith Miller and Ray Lindwall, both fit together for the first time in Tests that summer and proving almost unplayable on a wet pitch in humid conditions, England found themselves four wickets down with the score reading 23. More worryingly, John Edrich and Denis Compton, two of England's more consistent batsmen in the series were among them.

Bradman the tactician was in his elements. As Compton faced up to Lindwall, the captain moved Morris to square leg. Compton hooked the next ball from Lindwall straight to

Morris who held a brilliant low catch. Bradman rushed up to Morris and said: "Well caught Arthur. You know why I put you there now. I remember he played that shot in 1938."

Ray Lindwall bowling

Len Hutton stood like Marius among the ruins of Carthage, watching in dismay as Lindwall scythed through the batsmen picking up 6 for 20 to skittle the English out for a scarcely believable 52. England's innings had lasted for all of two hours and ten minutes. Hutton's contribution was 30. Neville Cardus, never one to hold back on prose, called it "an innings of noble loneliness withstanding one of the finest pieces of fast bowling of our times."

Lawrence Kitchin, then a young boy, wrote in Len Hutton – Cricketing Lives, about watching Lindwall bowl that day: "When he turned and began his long, gradually accelerating run, the uncomfortable silence of the crowd was so complete that we seemed to hear the beat of his footsteps from the terraces."

When the Australians walked out to bat three hours later, it looked like they were doing so on a different surface. John Arlott would write: "If anyone retained any suspicion there was life in the wicket, Barnes and Morris at once removed it." Sid Barnes and Arthur Morris would put on an opening partnership of 117 and it looked like the capacity Oval crowd would have to come back the next day to watch Bradman bat. But little did they know there was another twist in the tale to come.

The Most Famous Ball in the History of Cricket

Eric Hollies, the reluctant Test bowler who had been drafted into the England squad at the Oval, almost hadn't shown up for the game, unwilling to miss two matches for his county Warwickshire to play in a Test where the rubber had already been decided. The Warwickshire Committee had finally prevailed upon him to play, a move that would change the course of cricketing history.

It all started at the stroke of six when Sid Barnes on 61 stepped out to Hollies, was beaten by a leg break and Godfrey Evans held on to the edge. Jack Fingleton captured the atmosphere as Barnes walked off and the small athletic figure of Bradman walked down the steps, the public enthusiasm bordering on the masochistic:

"Hundreds of people had queued all night. They had slept on wet pavements so that they could see the final appearance of Bradman, and his reception could not have been bettered. Though he had flayed them over the years with his bat, England's cricketing representatives still wanted more of Bradman. Like London during the blitz, they could take it."

Yardley had two messages in the middle. To his team, he said: "We'll give him three cheers when he gets on the

The tribute to Don Bradman as he walks in for his last innings

square." Then he turned to Hollies and said: "But that's all

we'll give him – then bowl him out."

To get the context to this conversation we need to go back to the Australian encounter with Warwickshire where Hollies had run through the top order. In the second innings of the match, with only 41 to get for a win, Bradman had walked out to the middle because he wanted another look at Hollies. The wily bowler was, however, no novice and knew better than to give the great man what he wanted. When he was thrown the ball, he first walked up to Test discard and teammate Dollery and captain Ron Maudsley to tell them that he was not going to bowl the googly. "I know I can bowl him with it, and I'll give it to him the second ball at The Oval."

Bradman describes in his *Farewell to Cricket* the next few moments as he faced up to Hollies:

"That reception had stirred my emotions very deeply and made me anxious – a dangerous state of mind for any batsman to be in. I played the first ball from Hollies though not sure I really saw it [It was a leg break he played off the back foot]. The second was a perfect length googly which deceived me. I just touched it with the inside edge of the bat and the off bail was dislodged." Hollies had delivered on his promise.

What no one on the ground had realised was that coming in to bat, Bradman had been four runs short of 7000 runs and he had been dismissed sixty-nine times in the past. The addition of those four runs would have taken his average, over the twenty years since his debut, past 100. The most untimely duck in the history of cricket was fated to immortalise the number 99.94.

Bradman was cheered all the way back to the pavilion. No duck in cricket had roused more emotion. Godfrey Evans reflected: "What is a nought in such a fabulous career, even such a nought at such a time?" A bemused Eric Hollies turned to Jack Young and mouthed: "Best f-ing ball I've bowled all season, and they're clapping him!"

There was dead silence in the dressing room when Bradman walked in. No one wanted to look him in the eye.

Sid Barnes walked up to him and said: "Got your whole innings on film, skipper." Bradman laughed. It was the end of an era, and no dramatist could have scripted it better.

Completing the formalities at the Oval

Resuming on a Monday morning at 153 for 2, Australia batted on through the day. The man in charge was Arthur Morris, steady, determined, imparting lessons on how to play off the back foot. His confidence grew as the overs went by, often dispatching pitched outside off to the leg side, forcing bowlers to change their line, even taking Hollies to the cleaners. The innings ended the only way it could – with Morris being run out trying to shield Tallon from facing Hollies. His brilliant innings of 196 ensured Australia finished at 389, leaving England in deficit by 337 in the first innings.

From the moment Hutton and Dewes walked into bat, the English had their backs to the wall. Other than a fighting, defiant 64 from Hutton there was little to speak of in England's second knock. Long before the innings folded up for 188, the result of the Test match had been painfully obvious to one and all. Now only the formalities remained.

In the post-match speech, Bradman confirmed this would be his last Test and Yardley made a gracious reply reflecting the thoughts of his countrymen: "Future Australian sides will seem strange without Don Bradman. The only people who can be happy about his Test retirement are those who face the task of getting him out."

The Tryst with Invincibility

The Test series was over, invincibility beckoned, but she was yet an untamed tigress, and no one knew that better than Don Bradman. With five first-class and two second-class matches to go, for the 1948 team, there would be no let-up.

After a rare day off, the team travelled to Canterbury to play Kent. Over two Ashes series, Godfrey Evans had stood behind the stumps while Bradman scored over 1400 runs, and not once had been involved in a dismissal of the great man. Against Kent, batting in his fifties, Bradman edged a ball, and Evans failed to appeal. After the day's play, with a laugh, Bradman told Evans: "You are a fool, Godfrey; you've been trying to get me out all these years and you threw away the perfect chance out there."

When Kent batted, Evans' teammates teased him that they would at least get more than 52. As it turned out, they got 51. Australia won by an innings and 186 runs. Over the next few days first, the Gentlemen of England and then Somerset were disposed of, each by an innings. The match against the South of England ended in a rare draw.

And then came the Scarborough Festival Game, the last first-class game of the tour and one that had spoilt the records of Warwick Armstrong's 1921 team and Bradman's own 1938 side. As far as the Australians were concerned, it was a trap waiting to be sprung. Laveson-Gower chose a team with six players from the current England side and the rest were retired English Test players. Bradman countered with a full-strength Australian Test team.

As things turned out, Bradman need not have worried so much. Lindwall ran through the batting, the hosts scoring only 177. The Australians replied with 489 for 8 declared, Bradman gifting his wicket away at a personal score of 151 and running into the pavilion as the catch was taken in the outfield. The weather ensured that the match ended in a draw.

While no one would have grudged the invincibility label after this match, the last one in England, Bradman was not one for unfinished tasks. He played in the last two matches in Scotland, his team winning both by an innings, and Bradman sealed the win in the final fixture, his last match in Britain, with a brilliant 123.

For the first and indeed last time in the history of the Ashes, an Australian team had gone undefeated through an entire tour of the British Isles. It had not been easy, but employing great determination, courage, undeniable talent and ruthlessness when required, Don Bradman and his 1948 team had truly earned the sobriquet that would remain exclusively theirs – *The Invincibles*.

Scorecard - 5th Test

England v Australia

	Australia in British Isles 1948 (5th Test)
Venue	Kennington Oval, Kennington on 14th, 16th, 17th, 18th August 1948 (5-day match)
Balls per over	6
Toss	England won the toss and decided to bat
Result	Australia won by an innings and 149 runs
Umpires	HG Baldwin, D Davies
Close of play day 1	Australia (1) 153/2 (Morris 77*, Hassett 10*)
Close of play day 2	England (2) 54/1 (Hutton 19*, Edrich 23*)
Close of play day 3	England (2) 178/7 (Yardley 2*)

England first innings

		Runs	Balls	Mins	4s	6s
L Hutton	c Tallon b Lindwall	30	124	147	1	-
JG Dewes	b Miller	1	6	5	-	-
WJ Edrich	c Hassett b Johnston	3	20	20	-	-
DCS Compton	c Morris b Lindwall	4	9	11	-	-

JF Crapp	c Tallon b Miller	0	19	23	-	-
*NWD Yardley	b Lindwall	7	31	33	-	-
AJ Watkins	lbw b Johnston	0	16	16	-	-
+TG Evans	b Lindwall	1	9	4	-	-
AV Bedser	b Lindwall	0	3	5	-	-
JA Young	b Lindwall	0	4	5	-	-
WE Hollies	not out	0	12	8	-	-
Extras	(6 b)					6
Total	(all out, 42.1 overs)					52

Fall of wickets:

1-2 (Dewes), 2-10 (Edrich), 3-17 (Compton), 4-23 (Crapp), 5-35 (Yardley), 6-42 (Watkins), 7-45 (Evans), 8-45 (Bedser), 9-47 (Young), 10-52 (Hutton, 42.1 ov)

Australia bowling	Overs	Mdns	Runs	Wkts	Wides	No-Balls
Lindwall	16.1	5	20	6	-	-
Miller	8	5	5	2	-	-
Johnston	16	4	20	2	-	-
Loxton	2	1	1	0	-	-

Australia first innings		Runs	Balls	Mins	4s	6s
SG Barnes	c Evans b Hollies	61		126		
AR Morris	run out	196		406	16	-
*DG Bradman	b Hollies	0	2	1	-	-
AL Hassett	lbw b Young	37		134		
KR Miller	st Evans b Hollies	5				
RN Harvey	c Young b Hollies	17				
SJE Loxton	c Evans b Edrich	15				
RR Lindwall	c Edrich b Young	9				
+D Tallon	c Crapp b Hollies	31				
DT Ring	c Crapp b Bedser	9				
WA Johnston	not out	0	2	1		
Extras	(4 b, 2 lb, 3 nb)					9
Total	(all out, 158.2 overs)					389

Fall of wickets:

1-117 (Barnes), 2-117 (Bradman), 3-226 (Hassett), 4-243 (Miller), 5-265 (Harvey), 6-304 (Loxton), 7-332 (Lindwall), 8-359 (Morris), 9-389 (Tallon), 10-389 (Ring, 158.2 ov)

England bowling	Overs	Mdns	Runs	Wkts	Wides	No-Balls
Bedser	31.2	9	61	1	-	1
Watkins	4	1	19	0	-	-
Young	51	16	118	2	-	-
Hollies	56	14	131	5	-	1
Compton	2	0	6	0	-	1
Edrich	9	1	38	1	-	-
Yardley	5	1	7	0	-	-

England second innings		Runs	Balls	Mins	4s	6s
JG Dewes	b Lindwall	10				
L Hutton	c Tallon b Miller	64				
WJ Edrich	b Lindwall	28				
DCS Compton	c Lindwall b Johnston	39				
JF Crapp	b Miller	9				
*NWD Yardley	c Miller b Johnston	9				
AJ Watkins	c Hassett b Ring	2				
+TG Evans	b Lindwall	8				

AV Bedser	b Johnston	0	5	5	-	-
JA Young	not out	3	7	10	-	-
WE Hollies	c Morris b Johnston	0	1	1	-	-
Extras	(9 b, 4 lb, 3 nb)					16
Total	(all out, 105.3 overs)					188

Fall of wickets:

1-20 (Dewes), 2-64 (Edrich), 3-125 (Compton), 4-153 (Hutton), 5-164 (Crapp), 6-167 (Watkins), 7-178 (Evans), 8-181 (Bedser), 9-188 (Yardley), 10-188 (Hollies, 105.3 ov)

Australia bowling	Overs	Mdns	Runs	Wkts	Wides		No-Balls
Lindwall	25	3	50	3	-	-	
Miller	15	6	22	2	-		1
Loxton	10	2	16	0	-	-	
Johnston	27.3	12	40	4	-	-	
Ring	28	13	44	1	-		2

Notes

--> The match was scheduled for five days but completed in four.
--> JG Dewes made his debut in Test matches
--> AJ Watkins made his debut in Test matches
--> SG Barnes made his last appearance in Test matches
--> DG Bradman made his last appearance in Test matches
--> AR Morris (1) passed his previous highest score of 182 in Test matches
--> L Hutton (2) passed 2000 runs in first-class matches for the season when he reached 37
--> AJ Watkins made his debut for England in first-class matches
--> DT Ring made his debut in England in Test matches
--> KR Miller reached 50 wickets in first-class matches for the season when he dismissed JF Crapp, his 2nd wicket in the England first innings
--> WA Johnston reached 150 wickets in first-class matches when he dismissed AJ Watkins, his 2nd wicket in the England first innings
--> KR Miller reached 150 wickets in first-class matches when he dismissed JF Crapp, his 2nd wicket in the England first innings
--> DT Ring reached 50 wickets in first-class matches for the season when he dismissed AJ Watkins, his 1st wicket in the England second innings

Scorecard Courtesy: www.cricketarchive.com

My Encounters with the Invincibles

By Kersi Meher-Homji

My interest in cricket started only in 1950 when I heard on a neighbour's radio India's great batsman Vijay Hazare scoring a century in an unofficial Calcutta (now Kolkata) Test against a strong Commonwealth team.

That means I neither saw nor heard on radio any of the 1948 Test series in England involving the Australians under Don Bradman who did not lose a match on the entire tour of England that year and aptly called the Invincibles.

However, I did watch with awe and admiration three of the Invincibles – Ian Johnson, Ray Lindwall and Neil Harvey – play in Test matches in India a decade later.

Neil Harvey

I became a Harvey fan after watching the elegant left-hander score fluent centuries in the Bombay (now Mumbai)

Tests; 140 runs in 1956-57 and 102 in 1959-60. He remains as one of the most electrifying batsmen I have watched.

After migrating to Australia in 1970, I had closer contacts with some of the legendary Invincibles. Imagine my thrill and ecstasy when I first saw Neil Harvey with his wife at a shopping centre in St Ives, a suburb in Sydney. I hesitated for a few minutes but approached him and he responded in a friendly way.

I kept running into him at the St Ives Shopping Centre and later at meetings of Australian Cricket Society (NSW branch) and discuss cricket's highs and lows. But since his beloved wife passed away a few years ago his visits at the Shopping Centre have reduced. Even the mention of her name brings tears to his eyes.

Don Bradman

Love for his wife is what Neil Harvey shares with Don Bradman. I wanted to write a fan letter to Bradman for a long time but hesitated. He must be getting hundred letters a week so why should I add to his troubles. Then I asked myself, "why not write a short letter?"

I got Sir Donald's address from a Cricket Society friend and started drafting a letter to the great man. Should I start with "Dear Sir" (too formal) or "Dear Don" (too familiar) or "Sir Donald" … I decided on "Dear Don Bradman" and wrote from my heart; my admiration for him without sounding too sentimental.

I did not expect a reply but lo and behold I received his hand-written letter starting with "Dear Kersi". I received three more friendly letters but the fourth one was his last. "Regretfully, Jessie [his wife and sweetheart] and I are facing a daunting 1997 because of ill health but we shall face the future with hope and courage. Good luck to you and yours, Sincerely, Don Bradman (autographed)". Jessie passed away a few months later.

When I asked Neil Harvey, the baby of the 1948 team, as to how Bradman would have performed in today's cricket, he replied, "Don was a genius and would have excelled in five-day, three day or one-day cricket today. Besides being a brilliant, adventurous batsman, he was a marvellous fielder and a deep thinker."

Keith Miller

I was elated when Keith Miller, the legendary all-rounder, reviewed one of my books in Daily Telegraph on19 October 1980. He wrote, "India's Kersi Meher-Homji has written a fascinating book on cricketing families: the Chappells, the Harveys, the Benauds, the Bedsers and many others. Entitled Cricket's Great Families, it's the first of its kind and features 22 families. A nice Chrissie [Christmas] present for cricket enthusiasts."

I have preserved that faded clipping for more than 38 years.

Since then I had the good fortune to befriend this Australian cricket icon.

Tall and handsome, dashing and debonair with a mane of dark hair and nicknamed Nugget, Miller exuded sex and six appeal. According to his biographer Mihir Bose, "the pedigree of his stroke play rivalled [Wally] Hammond's."

It was his reputation as a six-hitter that made me approach 'Nugget' Miller. In 1996 I was writing my book Six Appeal and contacted him over the phone. He was then 75 and recovering from a mild stroke but talked in a friendly manner to a complete stranger.

He told me frankly, "Ask me anything on horse racing and classical music but not on cricket statistics. I am not a figures man." After a short pause he asked me to contact him half an hour later "so that I recollect my thoughts." When I rang him later he could recall his six-hitting sprees in 3-D effect.

"The one six I remember vividly was against England at the SCG [Sydney Cricket Ground]. I straight drove [England's] Alec Bedser and it went a long, long way and landed near the concrete stand. A straight six is the real thing, not a hook or a hoick to mid-on."

Now Keith was getting in top gear and reminiscing as if to an old mate.

"I'll tell you a funny story way back from the 1945 unofficial tour of England. I hit a straight six in the direction of BBC commentary room. Rex Alston, the famous English commentator, was on air then and I was told his description went like this: 'Miller has hit the ball in the air, I think it is coming our way. IT IS COMING OUR WAY' ... and then crash, kaboom as the ball shattered the BBC's glass pane!"

Apart from towering sixers, Miller also specialised in 'ponders' – dispatching balls into ponds and rivers. He recalled belting soaring sixes at Eden Gardens, Calcutta, in an unofficial test match against India in 1945-46.

"I borrowed a bat from team mate Dick Whitington as we crossed on the way to the crease. Knowing my penchant for smash hits, he asked me to be careful with his bat. I nodded and promptly drove Vinoo Mankad over the sightscreen for four sixes in two overs. All four sixes landed in a pond outside the ground. To Dick's relief, I was soon stumped!"

Miller's sixes twice sent spectators to hospitals during Australia's triumphant tours of England in 1948. The young men who were hit returned home safely after having tasted possibly their only brush with fame. Brush with fame? More like a double bang! After retirement both Whitington and Miller turned journalists and co-authored popular books Cricket Caravan, Straight Hit and Gods or Flannelled Fools among others.

He recalled to me belting two more sixes in their watery grave while touring South Africa in 1949-50. At Port Elizabeth against Eastern Province he hit six sixes in his breezy 131. On jogging his memory, he said, "Oh yes, I remember reaching my ton with a six, one of the nicest and longest sixes I ever hit. It cleared the grandstand and landed in a pond in the park outside the ground. It was one of the shots that clicked."

He told me many other exciting stories which are included in my book Six Appeal, published in 1996. When the book was published I presented him a copy. It delighted him and I received a letter full of praises.

He passed away in October 2004, aged almost 85. More than thousand mourners filled Melbourne's St Paul's cathedral to farewell Australia's greatest all-rounder. All Australian cricketers wore black armbands during the second Test against India at Chennai.

To me, 'Nugget' Miller was more than a cricketer. He was Tarzan and Superman rolled into one.

Ernie Toshack

Now to the last Invincible I was friendly with, visiting at his home in Sydney few times. I would call Ernie Toshack and his wife Kathleen as good friends.

In 1994 I was researching on India's inaugural Test in Brisbane in November-December 1947 and was impressed by a bowler's figures of 2.3-1-2-5 and 17-6-29-6. Wow, 11 wickets for 31 runs in 19.3 overs as India tumbled for 58 and 98.

No, this destroyer was neither Ray Lindwall nor Keith Miller but a left-arm medium-pacer / spinner named Ernie Toshack. In 1946 he had similar spell-binding figures of 19-13-12-4 and 10-5-6-2 (that is, 6 for 18 in 29 overs) against New Zealand at Wellington, rolling out the Kiwis for 42 and 54.

Although these bowling figures had taken place 50 years ago, I got obsessed to meet and interview this forgotten hero. I somehow managed to get his address and organised an interview at his immaculate home in Sydney. Both Ernie and his wife Kathleen welcomed me, a complete stranger, with smiles.

He was 80 then but fit as he showed his vegetable patch maintained by him despite arthritis in his fingers. After that he showed me the deluxe edition of *Images of Bradman*, priced then at A$ 650 but received as a gift from Don.

"After Bradman, I have the highest regards for England's batsmen Wally Hammond, Denis Compton, Len Hutton, Cyril Washbrook and India's superb batsman who scored centuries in both innings of the 1948 Adelaide Test [Vijay Hazare]." This is quoted in Anindya Dutta's website www.cricketwriter.com

He remembered the Brisbane Test against India in 1947. "India was caught on a wet and drying pitch. Bowling spin, I took the last five wickets for two runs in 15 balls" he remembered showing me the mounted ball with an inscription.

Like Shane Warne he could bowl accurately for hours; both were crowd-pleasers and match-winners. "Your opinion of Warne?" I asked.

"Warne spins the ball as I've never seen anyone spin before. Richie Benaud and Bill O'Reilly were also excellent spinners. Garry Sobers was a grand all-rounder and a nice chap. When we were introduced he told me that when he was a boy he was nicknamed 'Toshack' because he also bowled left-arm fast-medium and slow."

Toshack was born in 1914 in Cobar, a mining town in New South Wales. He was one of five children and was orphaned at six. He was brought up by aunts in different parts of NSW where he played cricket and rugby league. When schooling in Lyndhurst, he met Kathleen who he married over 50 years ago. A perfect hostess, she kept our interview going with cups of tea and sandwiches and an occasional memory jog for Ernie.

Tall, dark and handsome when young, he came to Sydney to further his cricket career. I asked him the reason for his nickname Black Prince. He reminisced with a chuckle, "During the tour of England in 1948, a lady looked in my direction and told her companion: 'He looks like a prince, doesn't he?' Keith Miller heard her and gave me the Black Prince nickname," he chuckled, now resembling a fair gallant knight!

I asked him as to how good Don Bradman was as a captain and person. He replied: "I could not speak too highly of him. He was a great captain and you couldn't find a nicer chap." In a personal letter, Bradman wrote to me a year later: "Ernie was always a good friend."

In England in 1948, Ernie took 11 wickets in four Tests including 5 for 40 at Lord's and surprised all by averaging 51 with the bat. Incidentally, he batted right-hand but bowled left-arm medium. The highlight of this tour was his adding 55 runs for the last wicket with Lindwall in the Leeds Test, sadly his last. He had to be hospitalised for a cartilage operation.

"Bradman advised me to be operated on in England because it would be free of charge. By a coincidence, I got the same surgeon who had operated on Bradman for appendicitis on the previous tour," he recalled.

Injuries at crucial stages hindered his progress to the top but his place in history as one of Bradman's invincible is assured. A steel plate with 14 screws in his left leg made a radiologist exclaim: "There is more iron in your leg than in the Sydney Harbour Bridge!"

This meeting was the first of two others. We exchanged letters and Christmas - New Year cards, written mostly by his wife Kathleen. Ernie passed away in May 2003 aged 88 and Kathleen a few years later. At their funerals their daughter Maria, granddaughters Felecia, Monique and Vanessa and great-granddaughters Violet and Lara treated me as if I was part of the family.

Till now one of the first Christmas cards I receive is from their daughter Maria and her husband Harvey Field.

I am indeed a very lucky man to have known the above four Invincibles personally. Neil Harvey, the only Invincible now alive, is 90. May he complete his century!

APPENDIX - 1948 Ashes Series

Most Runs

Player	Team	Matches	Innings	Runs	Ave	Highest Score	100s	50s
Arthur Morris	Australia	5	9	696	87.00	196	3	3
Denis Compton	England	5	10	562	62.44	184	2	2
Donald Bradman	Australia	5	9	508	72.57	173*	2	1
Cyril Washbrook	England	4	8	356	50.85	143	1	2
Len Hutton	England	4	8	342	42.75	81	0	4
Sid Barnes	Australia	4	6	329	82.25	141	1	3
Bill Edrich	England	5	10	342	31.90	111	1	2
Lindsay Hassett	Australia	5	8	310	44.28	137	1	0

Best Batting Averages
Minimum 100 runs and three innings

Player	Team	Matches	Innings	Runs	Average	Highest Score	100s	50s
Arthur Morris	Australia	5	9	696	87.00	196	3	3
Sid Barnes	Australia	4	6	329	82.25	141	1	3
Donald Bradman	Australia	5	9	508	72.57	173*	2	1
Neil Harvey	Australia	2	3	133	66.50	112	1	0
Denis Compton	England	5	10	562	62.44	184	2	2
Cyril Washbrook	England	4	8	356	50.85	143	1	2
Sam Loxton	Australia	3	3	144	48.00	93	0	1
Lindsay Hassett	Australia	5	8	310	44.28	137	1	0
Len Hutton	England	4	8	342	42.75	81	0	4

Most wickets

Player	Team	Matches	Wickets	Average	Best Bowling
Ray Lindwall	Australia	5	27	19.62	6/20
Bill Johnston	Australia	5	27	23.33	5/36
Alec Bedser	England	5	18	38.22	4/81
Keith Miller	Australia	5	13	23.15	4/125
Ernie Toshack	Australia	4	11	33.09	5/40
Norman Yardley	England	5	9	22.66	2/32
Jim Laker	England	3	9	52.44	4/138

Best Bowling Averages
Minimum nine wickets

Player	Team	Matches	Wickets	Average	Best Bowling
Ray Lindwall	Australia	5	27	19.62	6/20
Norman Yardley	England	5	9	22.66	2/32
Keith Miller	Australia	5	13	23.15	4/125
Bill Johnston	Australia	5	27	23.33	5/36
Ernie Toshack	Australia	4	11	33.09	5/40
Alec Bedser	England	5	18	38.22	4/81
Jim Laker	England	3	9	52.44	4/138

Printed in Great Britain
by Amazon